What is Environmental History?

What is Environmental History?

J. DONALD HUGHES

polity

First published in 2006 by Polity Press

Polity Press
65 Bridge Street
Cambridge CB2 1UR, UK.

Polity Press
350 Main Street
Malden, MA 02148, USA

ISBN-10: 0-7456-3188-6
ISBN-13: 978-07456-3188-2
ISBN-10: 0-7456-3189-4 (pb)
ISBN-13: 978-07456-3189-9 (pb)

A catalogue record for this book is available from the British Library.

Typeset in 10.5 on 12 pt Sabon
by SNP Best-set Typesetter Ltd, Hong Kong
Printed and bound in Malaysia by Alden Press

The publisher has used its best endeavours to ensure that the URLs for
external websites referred to in this book are correct and active at the
time of going to press. However, the publisher has no responsibility for
the websites and can make no guarantee that a site will remain live or
that the content is or will remain appropriate.

For further information on Polity, visit our website: www.polity.co.uk

Contents

1

Defining Environmental History

Introduction

What is environmental history? It is a kind of history that seeks understanding of human beings as they have lived, worked and thought in relationship to the rest of nature through the changes brought by time. The human species is part of nature, but compared to most other species we have caused far-reaching alterations of the conditions of land, sea, air, and the living plants and other animals that share our tenure of the Earth. The changes humans have made in the environment have in turn affected our societies and our histories. Environmental historians tend to think that the unavoidable fact that human societies and individuals are interrelated with the environment in mutual change deserves constant recognition in the writing of history. Speaking of the contribution that environmental history can make to other kinds of history, Donald Worster, a leading American environmental historian, said that it is "part of a revisionist effort to make the discipline far more inclusive in its narratives than it has traditionally been."[1] Historians should see human events within the context where they really happen, and that is the entire natural environment. The narrative of history must, as the American environmental historian William Cronon said, "make ecological sense."[2] The theme

1. Plowing rice paddy in Java, near Borobudur, Indonesia. Agricultural history is a subject closely allied to environmental history.
Photograph taken by the author in 1994.

of the interaction of human events and ecological processes has been operative during every chronological period from the origin of humankind to the present.

The environmental problems that received global attention during the last 40 years of the twentieth century and whose importance has only increased in the present century show the need for environmental histories that will help in understanding ways that humans have in part caused them, reacted to them, and attempted to deal with them. One valuable contribution of environmental history has been to turn the attention of historians to topical environmental issues that produce global changes, such as global warming, altering weather patterns, atmospheric pollution and damage to the ozone layer, the depletion of natural resources including forests and fossil fuels, the dangers of radiation spread by nuclear weapons testing and accidents at nuclear power facilities, worldwide deforestation, extinction of species and other threats to biodiversity, the introduction of opportunistic exotic species to ecosystems far from their regions of origin, waste disposal and other problems of the urban environment, pollution of rivers and oceans, the disappearance of wilderness and the loss of amenities such as natural beauty and access to recreation, and the environmental effects of warfare including weapons and agents intended to impact the resources and environments of antagonists. Although long enough to suggest the variety and seriousness of the changes that make up the contemporary environmental crisis, the foregoing list is, unfortunately, incomplete. It might seem that many of these problems have appeared only recently, but there is no doubt of their tremendous effect during the course of the twentieth century, and most of them had important antecedents in all the previous historical periods. Environmental historians have given attention to these contemporary problems, but they also realize that the relationship between humans and the environment has had a formative role in every period of history, from ancient times onward.

The Themes of Environmental History

Environmental historians are a varied group as far as their individual interests and approaches are concerned, their philosophies in regard both to historical methods and subjects and to the environment. Their choice of themes falls into three very broad categories: (1) the influence of environmental factors on human history; (2) the environmental changes caused by human actions and the many ways in which human-caused changes in the environment rebound and affect the course of change in human societies; and (3) the history of human thought about the environment and the ways in which patterns of human attitudes have motivated actions that affect the environment. Many studies of environmental history lay emphasis primarily on one or two of the themes, but perhaps most have something to say on all three themes.

An example of a book that deals with the three themes is Warren Dean's *With Broadax and Firebrand: The Destruction of the Brazilian Atlantic Forest*,[3] which is in some ways a model for the writing of environmental history. Dean begins by talking about the evolution of the forest itself, continuing with its influences on the people who came to live there. He describes the successive stages of removal of forest and its replacement by agriculture and industries, and analyzes the attitudes toward the forest and its development by inhabitants before and after European colonization, including such groups as plantation owners, scientists, politicians, industrialists, and conservationists. He blends the themes in virtually every chapter.

Let us briefly examine each of the three themes. The first theme considers the environment itself and its effects on humans. Environment can be understood to include the Earth with its soil and mineral resources; with its water, both fresh and salt; with its atmosphere, climates, and weather; with its living things, animals and plants from the simplest to the most complex; and with the energy received ultimately from the Sun. It is important to understand these factors and their changes in order to do environmental history, but environmental history is not simply the history of the environment. The human side of the relationship is always included. Geology and paleontology concern themselves with the study of the vast reaches of the chronology of Planet Earth before humans evolved, but environmental historians make these subjects parts of their narratives only insofar as they affect human affairs. This means that environmental history inevitably has a human-centered approach, although environmental historians are keenly aware that humans are part of nature, dependent on ecosystems, and not entirely in control of their own destiny. Indeed, environmental history can be a corrective to the prevalent tendency of humans to see themselves as separate from nature, above nature, and in charge of nature.

Studies of the influences of the environment on human history include such subjects as climate and weather, variations in sea level, diseases, wildfire, volcanic activity, floods, the distribution and migration of animals and plants, and other changes that are usually regarded as non-human in causation, at least in a major part. Usually environmental historians have to depend on reports by scientists for background when studying the impact of these factors, and often geographers or other scientists, when discussing the implications of their work, become in effect environmental historians. Some, such as Jared Diamond in *Guns, Germs, and Steel*,[4] argue that it is the general conditions of the environment, the scale and arrangement of land and sea, the availability of resources, and the presence or absence of animals and plants suitable for domestication, and associated microorganisms and disease vectors, that make the development of human cultures possible and even predispose the direction of that development. A near-exclusive emphasis on the formative role of the environment in human history has been termed "environmental determinism," an idea that has a long history of its own and will be discussed more fully later.

The role of diseases in history is an example of the theme of environmental influence. The idea that various illnesses arise from environmental conditions has been held at least since the time of Hippocrates, the father of medicine in ancient Greece.[5] Human activities have played a critical part in the spread of communicable disease, of course, but their horrendous inroads into unexposed human populations and the loss of life experienced as a result of the great plagues identify disease as a natural force that all too often has operated outside human control. William H. McNeill's *Plagues and Peoples* is a wide-ranging survey of this subject.[6] In one of the masterpieces of environmental history, *The Columbian Exchange*,[7] Alfred Crosby argued that a major reason for the success of the European conquerors of the Americas was that they inadvertently brought with them communicable diseases to which they had developed resistance by long exposure, but to which the "virgin" populations of the New World were disastrously susceptible. The Europeans found that they met less resistance from the decimated Native Americans, but also were deprived of the labor force that a larger population might have provided. They tried to fill the latter need by importing slaves from Africa who shared to some extent, along with the Europeans, a resistance to Old World diseases.

The second, and undoubtedly the dominant theme of environmental history in terms of the number of works written by environmental historians is evaluation of the impacts of changes caused by human agency in the natural environment, and reciprocally on human societies and their histories. The kinds of human activities included are some that provide basic sustenance, such as hunting, gathering, fishing, herding, and agriculture. Others provide for the increasingly complex organization of human settlements from villages to great cities, including the provision of basic materials by water management, forestry, mining and metallurgy. Technology and industries, affecting most human activities including warfare, have become more sophisticated and taken up more human energy as the centuries have passed. All these affect the natural environment in many ways, both positively and negatively, from a human point of view. Many of them make the environment more amenable to human use; but all cause other changes that can be damaging, such as deforestation and the resulting erosion, reduction of biodiversity through extinctions, desertification, salinization, and pollution. In recent decades, newly recognized damaging changes include radioactive fallout, acid precipitation, and global warming due to the effects of a growing concentration of carbon dioxide and other "greenhouse gases" in the atmosphere. These in turn make the environment less amenable to sustained human use. Some environmental historians describe the ways in which societies have tried to accentuate the positive changes and limit the negative ones through pollution control and conservation of natural resources, including the preservation of selected areas as national parks, wildlife reserves, etc., and the protection of endangered species. Others trace the course of political decision-making in regard to the environment, and the struggles between the environmental movement and its often powerful opponents.

Environmental historical studies may give attention to one or several categories of human action affecting the natural environment, and many of them will be noted in what follows in this book. It should be noted that there are varieties of history that study many of these types of human activity, such as urban history, history of technology, agricultural history, forest history, etc., and that many of them have questions and interests in common with environmental history. For example, forest history and environmental history share so much in approach that in the USA the Forest History

Society and the American Society for Environmental History have published a single journal together entitled *Environmental History* since 1996.

Works that emphasize the second theme are so numerous, and many are so excellent, that it is difficult to select only one or two for mention here, but the following are two books that study human impact on the environment and may serve as examples. Robert B. Marks in *Tigers, Rice, Silk and Silt*[8] shows how the expansion of rice cultivation, in part as an imperial policy aimed at meeting the needs of a growing population, and marketing changes including silk exports, transformed the landscape of an important segment of South China. John Opie wrote a study of a Great Plains aquifer, *Ogallala: Water for a Dry Land*, that shows how demands for water in the American West drove the tapping and depletion of an underground reservoir of fossil water that underlies a huge area of the high plains.[9]

A third theme of environmental history is the study of human thought about the natural environment and attitudes toward it, including the study of nature, the science of ecology, and the ways in which systems of thought such as religions, philosophies, political ideologies, and popular culture have affected human treatment of various aspects of nature. It is impossible to understand what has happened to the Earth and its living systems without paying attention to this aspect of social and intellectual history, which, as Donald Worster put it, is a uniquely human encounter "in which perceptions, ethics, laws, myths, and other structures of meaning become part of an individual's or group's dialogue with nature."[10]

A notable book that investigates attitudes to the environment is Roderick Nash's *Wilderness and the American Mind*,[11] often used in environmental studies classes in the United States, first published in 1967 and in its fourth edition as of 2001. Nash discusses many varied attitudes, positive and negative, of European-Americans toward nature and their effects on preservation and/or development of wild areas in North America, from their roots in Europe to the twentieth century. It must be noted that he shows the ways in which Native American Indians appeared to the European-Americans, but does not attempt to examine their own views of nature. American Indian environmental views are explored in *North American Indian Ecology* by J. Donald Hughes.[12]

Many environmental historians maintain that what people think and believe exerts a motive force on how they will behave in regard to the natural world. Others point out that people are skillful at adapting their attitudes, whether enjoined by commandments or developed through personal philosophies, to their needs and desires, and that this is as true of the environmental sphere as any other.

Among the Scholarly Disciplines

Environmental history, as John McNeill succinctly put it, "is about as interdisciplinary as intellectual pursuits can get."[13] With interests in matters that often cross the usual subject boundaries, including the formidable and seldom-bridged chasm between the humanities and the sciences, environmental historians find themselves gathering information from widespread specialties and reading books that historians ordinarily have neglected or avoided. At the same time, as we have already noted, scholars from a number of disciplines have been caught up in environmental history and have often done a very good job of writing it themselves. The writing of environmental history is not always even limited to historians. To a degree uncommon for most other historical subjects, books on environmental history are written by authors from other disciplines such as geography, philosophy, anthropology, and biology. The following sections will comment on the relationship of environmental history to the social sciences, the humanities, and the natural sciences including ecology.

Related to other social sciences

History is a discipline sometimes regarded as one of the social sciences. Environmental history, as a subdiscipline of history, can also be considered in this way because it is in one sense the study of how human societies have related to the natural world through time. Donald Worster, in his influential essay, "Doing Environmental History," treated environmental history as an innovative movement within the discipline of history, but the three "clusters of issues" he notes as its major themes each draw "on a range of outside disciplines."[14] The Australian historical geographer J. M. Powell counters that environmental history is not a subdiscipline of history, but an interdisciplinary methodology.[15] There is empirical evidence, at least, for Powell's assertion, in that even the environmental historians most closely identified with the historical profession admit that much valuable work, and not a small proportion of all work in environmental history, has been done by scholars who have their roots in other disciplines.

William Green observes that no approach to history is more perceptive of human interconnections in the world community, or of the interdependence of humans and other living beings on the planet.[16] Environmental history, he adds, supplements traditional economic, social, and political forms of historical analysis.

This may be the result of the interdisciplinary nature of the subject itself, since to do environmental history properly requires familiarity with ecology and other sciences, the history of science and technology, and geography and other branches of the social sciences and humanities. There are several historical fields so closely allied to environmental history that a rigid line of separation cannot always be drawn. Further, as Stephen Dovers remarked, "It is hard to define the boundary between historical geography and environmental history."[17] Historical geographers discovered that they shared a border with environmental history, a border that they crossed with impunity, writing some fine environmental history. Among the geographers who have done so is Ian Gordon Simmons, whose *Changing the Face of the Earth: Culture, Environment, History* (1989)[18] is a brief, technically based review of the subject that considers varying rates of environmental change, problems of prediction, and issues affecting policy decisions and execution. Also, his *Environmental History* (1993)[19] is a valuable overview stressing the scientific bases of historical study. Andrew Goudie's useful text, *The Human Impact on the Natural Environment* (2000), has reached its fifth edition.[20]

The ecological paradigm was applied to the social sciences in a series of essays edited by Riley Dunlap in 1980. He noted that the social sciences largely ignored the fact that human societies depend on the biophysical environment for their survival, and exempted humans from the ecological principles that govern all other forms of life.[21] As a corrective, he and other authors applied models derived from ecology to their own disciplines: sociology (William Catton, Jr. and Dunlap),[22] political science (John Rodman),[23] economics (Herman Daly),[24] and anthropology (Donald Hardesty).[25] History was not represented, but a growing number of historians such as William McNeill[26] and Alfred Crosby,[27] were already considering how the ecological paradigm might transform our understanding of the human past and present.

A fully developed environmental historical narrative, properly speaking, should be an account of changes in human

2.   Sheep grazing on denuded land in the Navajo Reservation, Utah, USA. This illustrates one of the forms of environmental degradation analyzed by environmental history.
     Photograph taken by the author in 1963.

society as they relate to changes in the natural environment. In this way, its approach is close to those of the other social sciences such as anthropology, sociology, political science, and economics. One good example of this would be Alfred Crosby's *The Columbian Exchange*, which showed how the European conquest of the Americas was more than a military, political, and religious process, since it involved invasion by European organisms including domestic species and opportunistic animals such as rats. European plants, whether cultivated ones or weeds, crowded or replaced native ones, and the impact of European microorganisms on the indigenous population was even more devastating than warfare.

A very important thrust in environmental history is the study of political expressions of environmental policy. Many nations have embodied this in the creation of a body of environmental law, administrative departments such as environmental ministries, and governmental arms entrusted with the enforcement of environmental protection. The struggle to enact legislation in this field is also part of the story, with environmental organizations on one side and interest groups on the other. A good study in this area examining the structure of politics and the results of policy in the United States is *A History of Environmental Politics since 1945* by Samuel P. Hays.[28]

Environmental history is also related to economics. The "eco-" in economics comes from the same root as the "eco-" in ecology. Economics, trade, and world politics are regulated, whether humans wish it or not, and whether or not they are conscious of it, by the availability, location, and finite nature of what, in a language derived from economics, are called "natural resources."

Related to other humanistic inquiries

Like history itself, on the other hand, environmental history is also a humanistic inquiry. Environmental historians are interested in what people think about the natural environment, and how they have expressed their ideas of nature in literature and art. That is, at least in one of its aspects, environmental history can be a subfield of intellectual history. If this inquiry is to remain history rather than philosophy, it should never stray too far from the question of how attitudes and concepts affect human actions in regard to natural phenomena. However, it is also a perfectly valid part of the environmental historical enterprise to establish what the significant views were on the part of individuals and societies. One of the finest achievements in this area was Clarence Glacken's *Traces on the Rhodian Shore,*[29] which examined three major environmental ideas in Western literature from ancient times to the eighteenth century. Those ideas were that the cosmos is designed, that the environment shapes human beings, and that humans alter the environments in which they live, whether for good or ill. The roles of various religious and cultural traditions in encouraging or inhibiting practices affecting the environment have been the subject of much commentary and argument. A much-noted controversial example is Lynn White's article, "The Historical Roots of Our Ecologic Crisis,"[30] which argued that Medieval Latin Christianity, as a religion that exalted humankind over nature, prepared the way for Western science, technology, and environmental destruction.

Related to the natural sciences

Environmental changes are frequently held to be the result of climatic variations over the decades or centuries, and have been the subject of study over the past generation or two. For example, in France Emmanuel Le Roy Ladurie wrote *Times of Feast, Times of Famine: A History of Climate since the Year 1000.*[31] Reliable records of weather observations do not date back more than 200 to 300 years or so, and in most locations not that far, but recently data on historical climates have emerged from sources as diverse as tree rings in species in the temperate zones, and air trapped in the accumulated layers of snow in the ice caps of Antarctica and Greenland. Hubert H. Lamb and his Climate Research Institute in the UK were pioneers in climatic studies.[32] Christian Pfister and associates in Switzerland and Western Europe have mined written sources for hints on European climate in times from the Middle Ages onward.[33] Recently, several scholars, including Richard Grove, have engaged in lively speculation about how a phenomenon such as the Pacific warming cycle called the El Niño Southern Oscillation (ENSO) affects the activities of people even at great distances, and may have had a role in many historical events.[34] Environmental historians are concerned by the need to differentiate the effects of climatic change on the environment from those caused by human agency. Are the retreat of forests and the advance of the desert in North Africa in Roman times and afterwards mainly due to a dryer climate or to tree cutting, stream diversion, and grazing of goats by the inhabitants?[35] As information on climatic change becomes better and more available, it may be possible to give balanced answers to questions like these.

Environmental history derived to an important extent from recognition of some of the implications of ecological science on the understanding of the history of the human species. A herald who called forth a response across the crevasse of the two cultures, science and the humanities, was Paul Sears, who, in 1964, published an essay provocatively entitled "Ecology – A Subversive Subject." In it, he pointed out

> that the view of nature derived from ecological studies called into question some of the cultural and economic premises widely accepted by Western societies. Chief among these premises was that human civilizations, particularly of advanced technological cultures, were above or outside of the limitations, or "laws" of nature.[36]

Ecology, in contrast, placed the human species within a web of life, dependent on cycles of food, water, minerals, air, and on constant interactions with other animals and plants. Sears called ecology "the subversive science," and it has certainly subverted the accepted view of world history as it was up to the twentieth century. Adopting his controversial adjective, Paul Shepard and Daniel McKinley published a collection, "The Subversive Science,"[37] in 1969, whose 37 articles from various disciplines contained two by Sears. Shepard criticized the paradigm of human mastery, underlining the absurdity of believing that "only men were found to be capable of escape from predictability, determinism, environmental control, instincts and other mechanisms which 'imprison' other life." It amazed him that "Even biologists, such as Julian Huxley, announced that the purpose of the world was to produce man, whose social evolution excused him forever from biological evolution."[38] Even environmental historians, however, have not always come to grips fully with the implications of ecology, particularly community ecology.

One of these implications is that the human species is part of a community of life. It evolved within that community by competing against, cooperating with, imitating, using and being used by other species. Humankind's continuing survival depends upon the survival of the community of life, and upon achieving a sustainable place within it. History's job includes examining the record of the changing roles our species has enacted within the biotic community, some of them more successful than others, and some more destructive than others.

Victor Shelford, a leading ecologist in the twentieth century, asserted, "Ecology is a science of communities. A study of the relations of a single species to the environment conceived without reference to communities and, in the end, unrelated to the natural phenomena of its habitat and community associates is not properly included in the field of ecology."[39] A similar assertion can be made about environmental history, where the species studied is humankind. To a large extent, ecosystems have influenced the patterns of human events. The activities of the human species, in turn, have to an impressive degree made them what they are today. That is, humans and the rest of the community of life have been engaged in a process of co-evolution that did not end with the origin of the human species, but continues in the present. Historical writing should not ignore the importance and complexity of that process.

What needs emphasis is that all human societies, everywhere, throughout history, have existed within and depended upon biotic communities. This is true of huge cities as well as small farming villages and hunter clans. The connectedness of life is a fact. Humans never existed in isolation from the rest of life, and could not exist alone, because they are only one part of the complex and intimate associations that make life possible. The task of environmental history is the study of human relationships, through time and subject to frequent and often unexpected changes, with the natural communities of which they are part. The idea of environment as something separate from the human, and offering merely a setting for human history, is misleading. The living connections of humans to the communities of which they are part must be integral components of the historical account.

As Aldo Leopold wrote,

> One of the anomalies of modern ecolog[ical thought] is that it is the creation of two groups, each of which seems barely aware of the existence of the other. The one studies the *human community*, almost as if it were a separate entity, and calls its findings sociology, economics, and history. The other studies the *plant and animal community* and comfortably relegates the hodgepodge of politics to "the liberal arts." The inevitable *fusion* of these two lines of thought will, perhaps, constitute the outstanding advance of the present century."[40]

Environmental history is an active part of that fusion.

Environmental History and the Older History

Before the early decades of the twentieth century, historical writers regarded the exercise of power within human societies, and the struggle for it within and between human societies, as the proper subject of history. Thus wars and the careers of leaders dominated their narratives. It is significant that the first two great writers of history in the West, the Greeks Herodotus and Thucydides, each chose a war as his subject. Marxist historians turned their attention to the proletariat, the workers and peasants who did societies' labor, but, if the narrative added economics to politics, it was still the story of the power struggle in society. The older history, when it recognized that nature and the environment were present, treated them as a setting or backdrop, but environmental history treats them as active, formative forces.

More recently historians have turned to the hitherto obscured accounts of those who had seemingly lacked power: to women's history; the histories of racial, religious, and sexual minorities; even the history of childhood. It is an understandably tempting extrapolation to look at environmental history as part of this progression. In the pyramid of power, the beasts and trees, and Earth herself, occupy the lowest stone courses that support the structure. Historians can now demonstrate that these supposedly voiceless and largely defenseless entities were in fact authentic actors in the historical drama and include them, too, in the larger narrative. As ethical extension has granted roles to immigrants, women, and former slaves, and recently has considered whether trees should have rights,[41] so a similar historical extension can now grant narrative attention to other living things and the elements. It is true, as we shall see, that just as these other forms of history were largely outgrowths of social and political movements, environmental history's roots were intertwined with those of the conservationists and the environmental movement.

Environmental history cannot afford to ignore the realities of political and military power and the national, economic, and ethnic groups for whose ostensible benefits they are wielded. As Douglas Weiner announced in his 2005 presidential address to the American Society for Environmental History, "Every 'environmental' struggle is, at its foundations, a struggle among interests about power."[42] He pointed out that apparently rational programs for the preservation and/or improvement of landscapes entail one group being in control of the landscape, and almost as a rule, other groups being excluded, removed, or exploited. Stalin eliminated Kazakh herders to create the "virgin lands" for wheat farming in Central Asia, British imperialists transformed the subsistence economy of much of India into a landscape of exploitation and famine during the late nineteenth century,[43] and the creation of American national parks often involved the forced removal of Native American Indians.[44]

To see environmental history simply as part of a progression within the discipline of history would, however, be a serious mistake. Nature is not powerless; it is, properly considered, the source of all power. Nature does not meekly fit into the human economy; nature is the economy that envelops all human efforts and without which human efforts are impotent. History that fails to take the natural environment into account is partial and incomplete. Environmental history is useful because it can add grounding and perspective to the more traditional concerns of historians: war, diplomacy, politics, law, economics, technology, science, philosophy, art, and literature. It is also useful because it can reveal relationships between these concerns and the underlying processes of the physical and living world.

2

Forerunners of Environmental History

Introduction

Environmental history as a conscious exploration of human relationships to the natural environment in the past, that is to say, as a historical discipline, began in the late twentieth century and is one of the newest scholarly endeavors. However, the questions asked by environmental historians are in many cases very old ones that attracted the interest of writers from the Greeks and Chinese among other ancient peoples, through the centuries down to modern times. The themes of environmental history can be recognized in earlier thought: the influences of environmental factors on human societies, the changes in the natural environment caused by human actions and the effects of those changes in turn on human history, and the history of human thought about the world of nature and its workings.

The Ancient World

The first Greek historian whose work survives, Herodotus, recorded a number of remarkable changes made in the natural environment by human efforts, and generally reported the negative consequences of them. He believed that massive

3. The Artemis/Diana of Versailles in the Louvre, Paris, France, goddess of wild things and hunting. The ancients imaged gods and goddesses as aspects of the natural environment. Photograph taken by the author in 1998.

works like bridges and canals demonstrated an overreaching human pride that might call forth punishment from the gods. He wrote that when the Cnidians started to dig a canal through the neck of land that connected their city to the mainland in order to improve their defenses, the workmen suffered an unusual number of injuries from flying splinters of rock. Wondering why this was happening, they sent an embassy to ask the oracle at Delphi, who replied in direct words rather than her customary riddle: "Do not fence off the isthmus; do not dig. Zeus would have made an island, had he willed it."[1] The command to put down tools and cease work was duly issued. Similarly, disasters plagued the Persian king when he built a bridge of boats across the Hellespont strait (waves from a storm broke it), had his men dig a canal through the Athos peninsula, and when his army drank rivers dry and set forests on fire, all actions that disturbed the order of nature. When Cleomenes of Sparta set fire to a sacred grove and burned 5,000 Argive soldiers to death, Herodotus reports that some people believed that he was driven mad by the thought of divine punishment – for destroying a god's forest as much as for killing the men in a place of refuge – and cut himself to bits.[2]

Herodotus made scattered references to environmental impacts, but Thucydides, perhaps Greece's greatest historian, began his work by developing a theory of environmental influences on history. Because Attica, the district around Athens, had soil that was thin, dry, and relatively infertile, he maintained that its unattractiveness to potential invaders saved it from war and consequently preserved it from depopulation. Such relative safety made it a shelter for refugees fleeing from wars elsewhere, further increasing the numbers of people until they exceeded the capacity of the land to feed them. The leaders of Athens relieved this population pressure by sending out settlers to colonies on the Aegean and Mediterranean coastlands.[3]

Thucydides also constantly refers to the need of the warring Greek cities for natural resources, especially timber, which was essential for building ships and other military purposes. When the Spartans conquered Amphipolis, a northern colony of Athens, he says, "The Athenians were greatly alarmed ... The main reason was that the city was useful to them for procurement of timber for ship-building."[4] In another incident, the Athenian general Demosthenes gave the abundance of timber at Pylos as one reason for capturing the place, and in their counterattack, the Spartan sailors held back from landing on a rocky coast to save their ships' timbers. One way to get timber was to conquer forests; after his desertion, the Athenian commander Alcibiades told the Spartans that this had been one of the aims of the Athenians in launching their armada to invade Sicily.[5]

Although not a historian, the father of medicine, Hippocrates, advanced a theory of environmental determinism that is worth mention. In the work *Airs, Waters, Places*, he maintained that the health, temperament and energy of people living in a place are governed by its position in relation to solar exposure, prevailing winds, climate, and the quality of its water supply. He discusses the differences between Europe and Asia, and the characteristic cultures and susceptibility to diseases of a number of peoples known to the Greeks, relating them to the various environmental factors of their homelands.

Plato was aware of many environmental problems, and included advice concerning them in his ideal states in the *Republic* and the *Laws*. He also observed historical deforestation of the mountains of Attica in the *Critias*, offering archaeological evidence: large roof beams in huge buildings that still stood in his own day had been cut from mountains where only "food for bees" (flowering herbs and bushes) remained.[6] The former forest had served to store and release the rains, producing many springs, as evidenced by the shrines that stood at the same springs, dry in Plato's day. In the same period as the deforestation, massive erosion had removed the rich, soft soil, leaving only the rocky framework of the land, which Plato compares to the skeletal body of a man wasted away by disease.

An apt comparison may be made between Plato and the Chinese philosopher Mencius, who also lived in the fourth century BC and described deforestation in his homeland. A follower of Confucius, Mencius made many interesting comments on the human relationship to nature and gave some valuable advice on land management. He wrote one of the classics of Confucianism that were memorized by every schoolboy for much of the history of China and formed the mainstream of Chinese thought.[7] Consequently, he played a major role in creating the typical Chinese view of the environment and in influencing its treatment. A section of Mencius' book that has attracted the attention of modern environmental historians and forest historians is the description of Ox Mountain. It is an outstanding demonstration of the sage's acuteness in observing environmental change and its causes:

> Mencius said, "There was a time when the trees were luxuriant on the Ox Mountain. As it is on the outskirts of a great

metropolis, the trees are constantly lopped by axes. Is it any wonder that they are no longer fine? With the respite they get in the day and in the night, and the moistening by the rain and dew, there is certainly no lack of new shoots coming out, but then the cattle and sheep come to graze upon the mountain. That is why it is as bald as it is. People, seeing only its baldness, tend to think that it never had any trees. But can this possibly be the nature of the mountain? . . . When the trees are lopped day after day, is it any wonder that they are no longer fine? . . . Hence, given the right nourishment there is nothing that will not grow, and deprived of it there is nothing that will not wither away."[8]

Mencius had seen a mountain that had been denuded of its forests over the years by logging, and the way in which grazing can make deforestation permanent by preventing reproduction and the growth of small trees.[9] Mencius recorded two mountain ascents (of Mount Tai and the Eastern Mount) made by his model of sagedom, Confucius, speaking in terms that make it seem likely that he himself had climbed mountains.[10] There were undoubtedly many highlands in China that suffered the fate of Ox Mountain.

Another anthropogenic change in the landscape noticed by Mencius was the cultivation of wasteland.[11] Land management was an important topic that he considered to be one of the primary responsibilities of the state. He advised rulers to make periodic tours of inspection of their territory, and to use the condition of the land as prime evidence of the quality, or lack of it, of the stewardship of their subordinate noblemen. If the land was well cared for, such officers should be rewarded, but "on the other hand, on entering the domain of a feudal lord, if he finds the land is neglected . . . then there is reprimand."[12] The Greek historian Xenophon made a similar observation concerning the king of the Persians in the same century.[13] When the king traveled through any of his numerous and wide-flung provinces, Xenophon notes, he pointedly observed the condition of the land. Where a landscape was well cultivated and thickly planted with trees, he rewarded the local governor with honors and expanded territory; but where he found neglected fields, deforestation, and deserted lands, he removed the governor from office and replaced the miscreant with a better administrator. So the king judged the worth of his appointees by the care they gave to the land, and thus to its inhabitants, believing this to be just as important as maintaining a garrison for defense or a good flow of taxes. The principles seem clear: a governor who cares for the Earth and can cope with environmental problems can be trusted to govern well, and the quality of an administration can be judged by the state of the environment in its territory. Both Mencius and Xenophon recognized the principle that the authorities must rule on behalf of the inhabitants. "It is not enough, [Mencius] insisted, for a ruler to wish his people well; he must take practical economic measures to assure their welfare."[14] He stated this in the strongest terms, insisting that "the people are of supreme importance; the altars to the gods of earth and grain come next; last comes the ruler."[15] In theory, the ruler owned the land and parceled it out to those who used it, but rulers were not exempt from labor on behalf of the altars or the people. A landlord had to plow the land to grow grain for the sacrifices.[16] And it was the duty of the ruler in the administration of the land to care for it so that it would provide an environment to nurture native human goodness. The condition of the environment in a country offered the most telling evidence concerning the merit of its government.

To the environmental historian, one of the most distinctive emphases of Mencius must be his recommendation of conservation practices to ensure that resources would not be exhausted, but would be available to feed the people from year to year. In a crucial passage, Mencius said that Earth is more important than Heaven, and Man more important than Earth.[17] He seems to have grasped the basic principle of the sustainable use of renewable resources. His advice to King Hui of Liang is notable:

> If you do not interfere with the busy seasons in the fields, then there will be more grain than the people can eat; if you do not allow nets with too fine a mesh to be used in large ponds, then there will be more fish and turtles than they can eat; if hatchets and axes are permitted in the forests on the hills only in the proper seasons, then there will be more timber than they can use.[18]

Here it was assumed that regulations governing economic activities would be promulgated and enforced. The people should be allowed to work in the fields at seedtime and harvest, presumably not marched off to war. The nets with wide mesh to be used in fishery would allow the small fish and turtles to escape and grow to catchable size. A form of sustained-yield forestry would ensure a supply of wood in succeeding years. Mencius' advice concerning forest conservation was particularly sound. In the case of Ox Mountain, he observed the advance of deforestation and its causes. Speaking to King Hui, he advised careful practices of timber harvesting and the planting of trees, and in other passages, he objected to the building of huge mansions and indicated the wisdom of preventing the waste of cut logs.[19] As Herrlee Creel commented, "If the Chinese people had heeded Mencius' advice in this last connection, their economic position in the modern world would be considerably sounder."[20]

There is little comment approaching environmental history in Roman historical writing, although there are indications that forests had vanished from some districts. Cicero praised the ability of human beings to transform nature, including agriculture, domestication of animals, building, mining, forestry, and irrigation, summing it all up in a famous sentence, "Finally, by means of our hands we endeavor to create as it were a second world within the world of nature."[21]

Ibn Khaldûn (1332–1406) was a great Islamic philosopher of history whose works contain many references to the influence of the environment on human history. Born in Tunis, he lived in many places in western North Africa, and in Granada, Spain. His mature life was spent as a professor and judge in Cairo, Egypt. He made the pilgrimage to Mecca expected of all Muslims who are able to do it, and also happened to meet the feared Central Asian conqueror, Timur (Tamerlane), near Damascus. Timur liked him and allowed him to return to Cairo.

In his influential work, *Muqaddimah*,[22] Ibn Khaldûn described the various climatic zones of the Earth in terms reminiscent of the Greco-Roman geographer Ptolemy, and ascribed the characteristics of various human groups to environmental influence in ways that mirror the thought of

4. A small temple encloses a spring in the sacred grove of Karikan
    ("Dark Forest"), Uttara Kannada, Karnataka, South India.
    The practice of setting aside natural areas for worship is wide-
    spread in India and elsewhere, and has received attention from
    ecologists and environmental historians.
    Photograph taken by the author in 1994.

Hippocrates' *Airs, Waters, Places*. Like many Muslim scholars of the time, he was familiar with the Greek classical
writers. His most characteristic and original environmental
theory, however, concerns the influence of the desert on the
people who live there, the *badâwah* (Bedouin), and the contrast of desert folk with sedentary people of the towns. This
was not mere theory; Ibn Khaldûn had had many opportunities to observe desert peoples in North Africa. He said that
desert life keeps the people there from getting obese and

toughens them against famine. Members of desert tribes are "closer to being good" and more courageous than townsfolk, and rely on themselves rather than on the law and the defenses of cities.[23] The more firmly rooted in desert habits and the wilder a group is, the closer it comes to achieving a superiority over others. The desert way of life is prior to sedentary life, and is therefore the basis and reservoir of civilizations and cities. However, dynasties of rulers in cities, though derived from desert forebears, step by step lose their desert cultural attitudes and descend into extravagance and debauchery. Once cities are established, desert tribes become dependent on them for the necessities of life, and therefore are dominated by the urban population.[24]

Medieval and Early Modern Environmental Thought

Historical thought in the West during the Middle Ages was strongly influenced by the scriptural view that God guides history, and that nature is God's creation that has been given to man to use and to care for and reveals God's goodness. Monasteries were often built in wilderness areas, and monastic writers such as Bernard of Clairvaux observed the changing landscape, with fields and orchards replacing disordered wild growth, and men, many of them monks, controlling rivers, using the waters in irrigation and the energy in mills.[25] The changes brought about by human labor in the natural world were seen not only as useful, but also beautiful. Bernard lived in a period of widespread agricultural expansion, settlement, and forest clearance, however, and most of the work was done by ordinary peasants, not by monks.

Glacken notes that medieval historians of the northern barbarian peoples, such as Cassiodorus, Paul the Deacon, Isidore of Seville, and Jordanes, tended to give overpopulation and climate as reasons for their invasions of central and southern Europe.[26] The rigors of the cold northern climates, they thought, increased the vigor of the inhabitants and perhaps encouraged them to have children in numbers greater than their lands could support.

Changes in environmental legislation were sometimes sufficiently sweeping – and disliked by the common people – to be mentioned in medieval chronicles. For example, one of the anonymous scribes of the *Anglo-Saxon Chronicle* objected to the introduction of Norman forest law to England, creating vast royal forests and reserving hunting rights for the king:

He made great protection for the game
And imposed laws for the same,
That who so slew hart or hind
Should be made blind.
He preserved the harts and boars
And loved the stags as much
As if he were their father.
Moreover, for the hares did he decree that they should go
free.
Powerful men complained of it and poor men lamented it,
But so fierce was he that he cared not for the rancor of them
all,
But they had to follow out the king's will entirely
If they wished to live or hold their land,
Property or estate, or his favor great.[27]

Information about environmental changes in the Middle Ages is more likely to come from local histories than from general histories, since such changes were more often noted in the landscape of a single district. A law enacted to prevent pollution in an Italian city, for instance, is more likely to be mentioned in a history of that city than in a history of Italy, which would be concerned mainly with dynastic and military history.[28]

Richard Grove, in his groundbreaking study, *Green Imperialism*, has shown that scientists, including physicians, sent out by colonial powers as early as the seventeenth century, noticed environmental changes on oceanic islands, in India and South Africa – changes that were often so rapid that they could be chronicled within the span of a human life.[29] They recorded evidence of human-induced deforestation and climatic change. Although as a rule they did not present their findings in formal histories, they definitely provided impetus for the idea that humans have caused environmental alterations around the world, and that many of these changes represent not advance, but degradation. Many European students of botany, zoology, climatology, and geography came to serve as administrators or founders of research institutions. Among the latter, botanical gardens served an unusually important role in the growth of environmental theory. Colonial regimes appointed the directors of botanical gardens to other important positions, and made professional scientists advisors or even governors, and at times their ideas were heard and even given practical trials. Such cases may have been exceptional, however, since the governments and companies that sent the scientists preferred that they devote their efforts to projects with immediate economic returns, and punished those devoted to pure science by transfers and reduced appropriations. "States will act to prevent environmental degradation only when their economic interests are shown to be directly threatened," Grove observes. "Philosophical ideas, science, indigenous knowledge and threats to people and species are, unfortunately, not enough to precipitate such decisions."[30] Ironically, had those in power listened to the keen observers of nature, they might have profited in the long run. One of the more convincing arguments advanced by the early scientists was that it was in the interest of the colonial governments to prevent the degradation of the environment in the territories they controlled. "The state," as the economist Richard Cantillon had proposed, is "a tree with its roots in the land."[31] If the colonies were deforested, they could no longer supply timber. Deforested lands suffer erosion and decreased rainfall, so that both soil and water for food production and other crops will decline. Faced with poverty and famine, colonial peoples will become rebellious.

Where one might have expected to find apologists for imperialism, Grove discovers individuals who were keen observers, creative thinkers, and critical analysts of destructive methods and their application among the peoples and ecosystems Europe had come to dominate. Among these scientists, Pierre Poivre, the French commissaire-intendant of Mauritius in the mid-eighteenth century, noted the decline in rainfall that accompanied deforestation, and advised the preservation and restoration of the landscape, whose past treatment, wasting the assets of home nation and colony alike, had been "sacrilegious" since deforestation had placed the "land in servitude."[32] When first glimpsed, the islands had seemed to be Eden, but no longer. He offered a convincing justification for conservation, and tried to carry it out in practice. Thomas Jefferson was attracted to many of Poivre's ideas.

A few early environmentalists, arguing for the safeguarding and nurturing of the natural environment, were attracted to the Hindu and Jaina views of harmony between people and nature that they found in India. "The ability to equate the divine with 'all beings' marked a very significant departure from Western or biblical notions of order and the primacy of man in creation."[33] They showed interest in indigenous knowledge of biota and in earlier conservation practices such as the precolonial *shikargahs*, or wildlife and forest reserves established in Indian kingdoms. Often environmental concern on the part of colonial scientists went hand in hand with reformist sympathies for the welfare of local people, and even with feminist ideas. Grove sketches the careers of remarkable men such as the Scottish surgeon, naturalist, and botanist William Roxburgh, who connected ecological and climatic change in India to epidemics and famines, eventually articulating a general critique of the impact of colonial policies on the Indian people and environment. Some, like the surgeon Edward Green Balfour, were willing to alarm their associates and superiors not only with advocacy of conservation, but open anti-colonialism as well.

Among modern authors who helped turn attention to environmental history is George Perkins Marsh, who long served as US ambassador to Italy. He observed in the Mediterranean area and elsewhere "the character and extent of the changes produced by human action in the physical condition of the globe we inhabit," and warned in his great work *Man and Nature*,[34] published in 1864, that "the result of man's ignorant disregard of the laws of nature was deterioration of the land."[35] Differing from the prevailing economic optimism of the times, he saw "man" as the disturber of nature's harmonies. He observed that many human activities, such as deforestation, deplete the natural resources on which civilization depends. He suggested that this factor contributed to the downfall of the Roman Empire by creating a shortage of

5. The Pont du Gard, a Roman aqueduct that supplied the city of Nîmes (Nemausus), France, represents an achievement of Roman engineering. Water management is a major aspect of environmental history.
Photograph taken by the author in 1984.

supply of vital materials, especially fuels, with disastrous effects on the economic structure. *Man and Nature* was intended to be a worldwide survey of the ways in which humankind had damaged nature and continued to do so, and for him Rome was not the only civilized society that had experienced environmental crisis, but Marsh's familiarity with the Mediterranean countries, Europe, and North America led to an emphasis on those areas, and he said little except in general about the rest of the world. Marsh may be regarded as the first of the precursors to environmental history who systematically investigated the question of environmental deterioration and the possible exhaustion of natural resources.

Comparing the Earth to a house, Marsh aptly said, "We are, even now, breaking up the floor and wainscoting and doors and window frames of our dwelling, for fuel to warm our bodies and seethe our pottage, and the world cannot afford to wait until the slow and sure progress of science has taught it a better economy."[36] Earlier, he had said that due to the destructive activities of humankind,

> the Earth is fast becoming an unfit home for its noblest inhabitant, and another era of equal human crime and human improvidence, and of like duration with that through which traces of that crime and that improvidence extend, would reduce it to such a condition of impoverished productiveness, of shattered surface, of climatic excess, as to threaten the depravation, barbarism, and perhaps even the extinction of the species.[37]

Since he is so eloquent in portraying human destruction of the natural environment, it is too easy to mistake Marsh as a defender of untrammeled nature, but that is not his purpose. As he puts it, "[A]ll that I can hope is to excite an interest in a topic of much economical importance, by pointing out the directions and illustrating the modes in which human action has been or may be most injurious or most beneficial in its influence upon the physical conditions of the earth we inhabit."[38] Humankind may have waged ruthless war "on all the tribes of animated nature," but also has ennobled many of them through domestication. Wilderness for Marsh is either luxuriant but difficult to use, or dry and barren. He hopes for a world that contains a vigorous, thriving human community engaged in agriculture and all the civilized arts, and such a community cannot exist without transforming the landscape.

Marsh's most trenchant point is that many of the changes humans make in the natural environment, whether accompanied by good intentions or by disregard of the consequences, injure the environment's usefulness to humans. A forest on a mountainside should be maintained in a relatively pristine condition, not for the forest's sake, but in order to prevent erosion and to ensure a dependable year-round supply of fresh water. It is true that the forest and mountain are also beautiful, but aesthetics also represents a human value. One can discern in Marsh's approach a desideratum: a balance between man and nature in which man's needs are met and nature's harmonies are preserved. He believes that is possible: man destroys, but man can also be a coworker with nature, a restorer of disturbed harmonies.

The Early Twentieth Century

In the early and middle twentieth century, a group of historians in France, with some colleagues elsewhere, particularly traced the reciprocal influences of human societies and the environment on a global scale. As part of an effort to broaden the horizon of history, they emphasized the importance of geographical settings and, in addition to having wide influence on historians and geographers, provided the impulse that helped to stimulate environmental history. They are generally called the *Annales* school, after the title of the journal founded in 1929 in which many of their papers were published.

One of the founders of the *Annales* school was Lucien Febvre (1878–1956), Others prominent in the group were Fernand Braudel, Marc Bloch, Georges Duby, Jacques Le Goff, and Emmanuel Le Roy Ladurie.[39] Febvre's book, *A Geographical Introduction to History*, is a classic.[40] In it Febvre insisted that historians should recognize the importance of the environment, and of geographical studies, in their field. As such, it is one of the most important texts leading to the recognition of environmental history as a subject and method. Febvre argues, in opposition to some sociologists, that the natural environment does have an important relationship to human affairs. At the same time, he argues against environmental determinism. Many of the critics of a geographical approach to history charged that it made humans into pawns or "patients" of environmental forces. While Febvre insisted on the importance of the environment, he maintained that it did no more than establish "possibilities" for societies. Humankind, he insisted, had a broad range of choices within which freedom and creativity operated. Most environmental historians today would agree in general with this trend of Febvre's line of argument.

The philosophical portion of Febvre's book has lasting value both for historical and for contemporary understanding. His historical and anthropological examples, however, are sometimes dated or erroneous. The book is "human geography," not history *per se*, although much that Febvre says is of great value to historians, and he clearly shows that the legitimate object of research is the relation of environment to society in its historic evolution.[41]

Febvre is surprisingly ecological in his approach for his time. He understands that humans are part of natural systems and must constantly relate to other parts of them. For example, he opines, "Then for the notion of 'Man' we have . . . substituted that of human society and endeavored to explain the true nature of the action of such a society in its relations with the animal and plant communities which occupy the various regions of the earth."[42] Humans operate under the same, or similar, constraints as do animals and plants. However, he mentions few of what we today regard as environmental problems; there is a brief discussion of the deforestation of France, but almost nothing on pollution, loss of biodiversity, etc. Still, he is aware that human activities are damaging the Earth: "The civilized man directs his exploitation of the earth with a mastery which has ceased to astonish him, but which, when we reflect on it for a moment, is singularly disturbing."[43]

Early advocates of environmental influence often entertained the idea that climate and other environmental factors produce racial characteristics and differences. Febvre rejects racialist interpretations, but he treats them as dignified alternatives to his own. Also, he adopts stereotypes that are considered unacceptable today but they were part of the unthinking prejudice common in those years in Europe. For example, in describing African agriculture, he says, "The soil is not turned to any depth. The Negro merely scratches its surface."[44] His language is also sometimes sexist.

Fernand Braudel's study, *The Mediterranean and the Mediterranean World in the Age of Philip II*,[45] with its first edition in 1946, exemplifies the environmental emphasis in the *Annales* school. It is a history, but the first part of this two-volume, 1,300-page work is entitled "The Role of the Environment," and it begins with a section that proclaims, "Mountains Come First."[46] Following are many chapters on environment and economy, and subjects of traditional history do not appear until the second volume. Braudel offers a convincing and magisterial argument for the importance of geographical space and the environment to the history of the Mediterranean. He is aware of a changing environment, particularly a process of deforestation that advanced quickly, creating a shortage of wood for shipbuilding.[47] In Medina del Campo in Spain, he noted, because "the primeval forests of the Mediterranean were attacked by man and much, too much, reduced," due to its scarcity, wood for the fire became as expensive as the food it cooked in the pot for supper.[48] Changes in the climate, he believed, are often the result of changes caused by humans in the landscape. He connected a drying climate with "large-scale deforestation."[49]

A more extensive study of climatic change was undertaken by Emmanuel Le Roy Ladurie in his book, *Times of Feast,*

6. The braided channels of the Peneios River in Thessaly, Greece, are the result of erosion due to deforestation in the headwaters, a process that has been occurring since ancient times. Photograph taken by the author in 1966.

Times of Famine.[50] Using evidence from tree rings, dates of grape harvests, and depictions of the advances and retreats of glaciers in the Alps, Ladurie chronicled warm and cold periods including the Little Ice Age and demonstrated that climate is far from a constant in history.

Another impetus to environmental considerations in history came from American frontier historians such as Frederick Jackson Turner[51] and Walter Prescott Webb. Their theory held that the western frontier had provided an environmental safety valve that kept egalitarian enterprise alive, and the closing of the frontier around 1890 warned of social consequences. Webb described his method as an approach to history through geography and the physical environment.[52] James Malin's *The Grassland of North America* provided awareness of the ecological changes that accompanied the settling of the Great Plains.[53] It is hard to imagine any American historian of the mid-twentieth century who would not have been familiar with this strand of research. This is undoubtedly one reason why the United States was the theater for the initial appearance and development of environmental history as a self-conscious field of inquiry in the latter part of the twentieth century.

3

The Birth and Growth of Environmental History in the United States

Introduction

This chapter summarizes seminal developments of the field of environmental history in the United States, where it was named and first organized as a distinct subdiscipline of history. The early twentieth century saw the rise of interest in what was then called conservation history, which was concerned with the Progressive Conservation Movement and questions such as land use, resource conservation, and wilderness. The emergence of environmentalism after mid-century meant that historians turned their attention also to issues such as pollution, lifestyles, and environmental legislation. The chapter then briefly looks at a number of topics that have been prominent in US environmental historical writing, including overviews of American Environmental History, pre-Columbian developments, regional studies, biography, public history and legal studies, non-governmental organizations, the urban environment, environmental justice, and gender issues. Finally, fields where more specific environmental subjects were studied, and societies were set up, even before environmental history was a recognized subdiscipline, but whose practitioners have strong common interests with the latter, are mentioned, such as the history of technology, agricultural history, and forest history.

Between the late 1960s and the opening years of the twenty-first century, environmental history grew from a score of scholars scattered around the academic world, many of whom were unaware of one another, to a community of several hundreds or thousands, organized in several societies and well in touch through the Internet and a vast and rapidly growing body of published work contained in books and articles in a large and diverse number of journals. Those who have tried to survey the field, myself included, have soon found that their attempts to review the field comprehensively are overwhelmed by its size and its rapid exponential growth. John R. McNeill provided an admirable overview, "Observations on the Nature and Culture of Environmental History,"[1] in 2003, which is practically required reading for anyone interested in the subject, and modestly demurred that he had had to write "on the basis of a small sampling of the literature."[2] McNeill's sampling may have been small in relative terms, but not in absolute terms, as the range of the article, both wide and deep, demonstrates. I can only make an effort to follow in his footsteps, along with those of other trailblazers such as Alfred Crosby, Richard Grove, Samuel Hays, Char Miller, Vera Norwood, Joachim Radkau, Mart Stewart, Richard White, and Donald Worster.

American History from Conservation to Environment

Environmental history first emerged as a conscious historical effort in the United States in the 1960s and 1970s. This statement is not intended to deny that many of the themes of environmental history had already emerged in the works of European historians, a fact noted in the foregoing chapter, and which will be expanded in what follows. Also, attention had already been given by historians to the conservation movement in America, including the advocates of nature preservation such as John Muir, and the so-called Progressive Conservation Movement for prudent and scientifically based use of natural resources urged by such figures as John Wesley Powell and Gifford Pinchot. The Progressive

Conservationists had received the powerful support of the White House during the administrations of Theodore Roosevelt (1901–9) and Franklin D. Roosevelt (1933–45).

Historians of conservation saw the period from the "closing of the frontier" in 1890 to the Great Depression of the 1930s as a time of realization that the United States, particularly the West, could no longer be regarded as an inexhaustible mine of natural resources. Government policy changed from one of transferring land into private hands as quickly as possible to one of the creation of public land reservations to be administered by federal agencies. The US Congress had designated the world's first National Park, Yellowstone, in 1872, and a number of others followed, with the act establishing the National Park Service to administer them passing into law in 1916. The president had been given the authority to set aside Forest Reserves in 1891, and millions of acres were subsequently authorized, with Theodore Roosevelt taking such an enthusiastic role in the use of that authority that a conservative Congress revoked it, although perhaps too late, since Roosevelt made copious use of his pen before it was taken from him. All the same, under the US Forest Service, created in 1905, the national forest patrimony continued to expand. Other conservation efforts included wildlife sanctuaries, national monuments, soil conservation, water reclamation and irrigation, and the regulation of grazing.

A bird's eye view of US conservation history can be found in *The Quiet Crisis*, a book written in 1963 by Stewart Udall, Secretary of the Interior under presidents John F. Kennedy and Lyndon B. Johnson.[3] Udall portrayed the middle and late nineteenth century as a "raid on resources" by private exploiters, and the progressive conservation movement as a triumph of democracy in which resources under public ownership began to be used for the benefit of the people. Samuel P. Hays had offered a more critical analysis in *Conservation and the Gospel of Efficiency*,[4] in which he saw Rooseveltian conservation as an emphasis on scientific management and organizational efficiency. More recently, Adam Rome has reviewed the writing on US conservation history in "Conservation, Preservation, and Environmental Activism: A Survey of the Historical Literature."[5]

Roderick Nash, in *Wilderness and the American Mind*,[6] put conservation in the context of intellectual history, emphasizing preservationist rather than utilitarian thought, and set wilderness, as contrasted with urban locales or the "second landscape" of rural America, as the leading interest of some of the incipient American environmental history.

It was Hays, however, who defined the great change in American attitudes toward the environment in the period after the Second World War that gave birth to the environmental movement and to environmental history as a scholarly endeavor. In an article, "From Conservation to Environment: Environmental Politics in the United States Since World War II," later expanded in a book, *Beauty, Health, and Permanence*,[7] Hays noted the emergence of new environmental values, including the desire for environmental amenities, recreation, aesthetics, and health, all associated with rising standards of living and education. Of course Americans had been camping and hiking and generally enjoying the out-of-doors for at least half a century. John Muir had founded the Sierra Club in 1892 to promote wilderness values. Automobiles had become the leading form of transportation in the mid-1920s, carrying Americans to the parks and forests. But in the 1950s, free from the preoccupations of economic depression and war, they sought environmentally related recreation in unprecedented numbers.

Americans also had become concerned with environmental issues that directly affected them, beyond land use and resources. They had become aware of the dangers of radioactive contamination by fallout from nuclear bomb tests. Rachel Carson, in her 1962 book, *Silent Spring*, had warned of damage from persistent pesticides. News media told them of oil spills and water pollution in the Great Lakes, they had to deal with gasoline shortages, and they could see and feel higher levels of air pollution from the cities to the Grand Canyon. Emerging environmental movements reached nationwide awareness on the first Earth Day, April 22, 1970, a series of environmental laws was enacted by Congress and signed by presidents notably including Richard M. Nixon, and ecology, formerly a little-known science, became a household word.

It is undoubtedly the case that the historians who created the field of environmental history in the 1960s and 1970s were for the most part, if not overwhelmingly, environmentalists, and that this fact led them to choose that particular emphasis in their research and writing. Roderick Nash, for example, helped to draft a declaration of environmental rights and to organize a well-publicized conference on the issue in the aftermath of the disastrous 1969 oil spill in the Santa Barbara Channel, visible from his campus of the University of California, where he subsequently helped initiate an Environmental Studies program. From the beginning, however, they also demonstrated a concern that their work not be seen as a form of environmentalist journalism. John Opie addressed this issue in 1982, calling it "the specter of advocacy,"[8] in that environmental historians were then suspect within the historical community for promoting a point of view that might compromise their scholarship in a tendentious way. By and large, however, such mistrust was not warranted. Environmental historians guarded their objectivity (perhaps sometimes they overcompensated in their desire to avoid advocacy), and have often also been critical of environmentalists as well as their opponents. Opie also reminded his audience that advocacy has certain virtues, and that to avoid it completely may be to dodge important ethical questions. To be trenchant need not mean to be less committed. This is well exemplified by Donald Worster, widely respected as a historical scholar and perhaps the most renowned American environmental historian, who has never hesitated to recommend courses of action when they clearly derive from his informed understanding of history.

A group of scholars, mostly historians but including a significant proportion of philosophers involved in what was termed "environmental ethics," and scholars studying literature with environmental themes, formed the American Society for Environmental History in 1976 with John Opie as president. The journal of the society began publication in the same year, and was successively titled *Environmental Review* (1976–89), *Environmental History Review* (1990–5), and *Environmental History* (1996–present). The change in titles accurately reflects the gradual transformation of the society's scholarly efforts from a broadly interdisciplinary venture to one increasingly regarded as a subfield of history. Nonetheless, environmental history has remained from its conception a necessarily interdisciplinary endeavor everywhere that it is practiced.

Strands of Environmental History in the United States

A historiographical essay by Richard White entitled "American Environmental History: The Development of a New Historical Field," published in 1985,[9] gives an excellent overview of the nascent scholarship in the field. Since then, almost every author who has undertaken a historiographical review of environmental history in the US has complained that the vastness and diversity of the literature make any definitive claim of comprehensiveness impossible. A brief, insightful look at the issues that occupied the field in the 1990s is Mart Stewart's "Environmental History: Profile of a Developing Field." The most complete and trustworthy manual, however, is *The Columbia Guide to American Environmental History* by Carolyn Merchant, which appeared in 2002.[10]

In a book of this length, I cannot hope to emulate Merchant's admirable coverage. What follows here, therefore, is a brief look at texts in a few of the major subject areas that have attracted the attention of environmental historians in the United States in the years between 1970 and 2005. The works mentioned do not in any way exhaust the literature, or even the most important work on each subject, but serve only as selected examples that a student may find suggestive.

Merchant begins with "The American Environment and Native-European Encounters," which has precedence chronologically. An epoch-making book on the European invasion of the New World is Alfred Crosby's *The Columbian Exchange*.[11] Crosby attributed the success of the Europeans not just to superior weaponry and technology, but to the biological consequences of the organisms they brought with them, the "portmanteau biota" of animals and plants, and not least of all the microorganisms that caused "virgin soil epidemics" among Native Americans who had little resistance to them. The degree to which American Indians had ecologically friendly lifestyles has been a subject of controversy. Calvin Martin, in *Keepers of the Game*, maintained that their belief structure was adapted to the North American environment through long experience, but that it broke down under the impact of European trade and diseases, and that, in any case, Indian ecological virtues could not be appropriated by an alien Euro-American society.[12]

Granted the size and ecological diversity of the United States, an environmental history of the entire nation presents some of the same problems associated with world environmental history, which will be discussed in a coming chapter. Two texts, however, offer an excellent outline: *American Environmental History* by Joseph M. Petulla[13] and *Nature's Nation* by John Opie.[14] Still, the ecological limits of presenting a mainstream history are evident. Opie does a better job than Petulla in incorporating Alaska, but neither book mentions Hawai'i. Also see Ted Steinberg's more recent *Down to Earth*,[15] which is sharply critical of American capitalism's penchant for commodifying every aspect of nature.

Regional environmental histories appeared early and well represent the field, some regions more than others and not all regions are yet represented as such in the literature. But a region, more aptly than a nation, can be defined in ecological terms. The Great Plains had already emerged as the regional subject of the works of Walter Prescott Webb and James Malin mentioned in the preceding chapter.[16] The wider West was the subject of an earth-shaking 1970 article by Wilbur R. Jacobs, "Frontiersmen, Fur Traders, and Other Varmints: An Ecological Appraisal of the Frontier in American History,"[17] which helped to launch American environmental history on its way. Rather than brave explorers and openers of the West, Jacobs maintained, we should see the trappers and traders as raiders of the environment, for example, removing beavers from streams, which without their dams became open to erosion. In 1979, two important studies of the Dust Bowl, the ecological disaster of the 1930s, appeared, one by Donald Worster and another by Paul Bonnifield.[18] An earlier episode, the near-extinction of the bison, was placed in its ecological setting by Andrew Isenberg.[19]

7. A view of a section of the Great Plains from the air over Kansas, USA. The rectangular mosaic of land use is the result of the Federal Land Survey, beginning in 1785, and the Homestead Act of 1862. Environmental historians such as Donald Worster have written on the history of this region.
Photograph taken by the author in 1962.

An excellent guide to the environmental history of California, a state so large and varied as to be a region unto itself, is Carolyn Merchant's *Green versus Gold*.[20] This is a selection of original documents accompanied by brief interpretive essays on environmental transformations in every period of California's history. The voices of Native Americans, Spanish settlers, participants in the Gold Rush, foresters, farmers, water developers, urbanites, scientists, and environmentalists are included.

The early environmental history of New England was the subject of William Cronon's widely acclaimed study, *Changes in the Land*,[21] which traces the effect of European attitudes toward the land, and capitalism, on the transformation of the landscape and the removal of the Indians. Again, Carolyn Merchant, in *Ecological Revolutions*,[22] saw two major changes in New England land use, the first occasioned by the arrival of colonial families and the second by the shift to a market economy in the early nineteenth century. Richard Judd traced the origins of conservation in New England not to top-down government management, but to attitudes and decisions of common people.[23]

The environmental history of the South was skillfully analyzed by Albert E. Cowdrey in *This Land, This South*,[24] in which he pointed out the damage done by pests and soil erosion as a result of the widespread planting of single crops such as cotton, corn, and tobacco. Carville Earle responded in an article that defended the ecological role of southern small farmers.[25] A look at writing on the region is provided by Otis Graham.[26]

Biographies of important figures in the history of conservation and environmentalism form a component of US environmental history. Early figures such as George Perkins Marsh and John Muir received attention; Marsh's biographer is David Lowenthal.[27] Muir is honored by a number of biographies, among them ones by Stephen Fox, Michael Cohen, and Thurman Wilkins.[28] Steven J. Holmes' study, *The Young John Muir*,[29] is an environmental biography in a more specific sense, investigating the influence of Muir's environment on his intellectual development. The leaders of the progressive conservation movement have received biographical studies. Among them are lives of Gifford Pinchot by Harold Pinkett and Char Miller,[30] and looks at the conservation dimensions of Theodore Roosevelt by W. Todd Benson and Paul Cutright and Franklin D. Roosevelt by A. L. Riesch-Owen.[31] The dawning of the age of ecology is represented by Susan Flader's admirable study of Aldo Leopold, *Thinking Like a Mountain*,[32] and Linda Lear's definitive work on Rachel Carson.[33]

Histories of government agencies with responsibilities for, and/or effects on the environment, especially public lands, include the history of the US Forest Service as interpreted by H. K. "Pete" Steen, and a critical review of the checkered record of the same agency by Paul Hirt, *A Conspiracy of Optimism*.[34] The National Park Service was viewed critically, but in contrasting ways, by Alfred Runte and Richard Sellars.[35] Runte saw the motive for the parks as national pride rather than conservation, and Sellars argued that the agency had placed its management emphasis on recreational tourism rather than scientific investigation. Histories of individual national parks continue to appear. In this subject area, the interests of environmental historians often coincide with those of the growing field of public history. The National Council on Public History (NCPH) was founded in 1980, and works in Canada and other English-speaking countries as well as the US.[36]

In the period of dawning widespread environmental awareness and activism in the postwar period, the government began to enact legislation that moved beyond land management to broad environmental areas such as regulation of the pollution of air, water and soil, protection of endangered species, and visual landscape protection including the limitation of outdoor advertising. Environmental law soon became a recognized subject in legal education. It seems that at least until recently legal scholars have been more

8. The volcano Mount Rainier, elevation 4,392 m (14,410 ft) is the centerpiece of Mount Rainier National Park, Washington State, USA, designated in 1899. Many environmental historians have studied the history of national parks in the US and elsewhere.
Photograph taken by the author in 1970.

attracted to the study of environmental law than have environmental historians.[37]

Non-governmental agencies dealing with the environment are almost unbelievably numerous, which in itself may constitute a historical weakness of the environmental movement. One of the oldest, largest, and most powerful (although prone to schism) is the Sierra Club, which has occasioned several histories, including a friendly but honest one by Michael Cohen.[38] The politically complicated story of the Sierra Club's apparently successful campaign to prevent the building of dams within the Grand Canyon was proficiently researched by Byron Pearson in writing *Still the Wild River Runs.*[39]

Urban environmental history has proved to be a central theme in this increasingly urban nation. Martin Melosi is an astute and prolific writer in the field; three of his most noted books are *Garbage in the Cities*, on refuse management, *The Sanitary City*, on infrastructure, and *Effluent America*, on energy and related developments.[40] Joel Tarr, another pioneer of the urban environment, has written a masterpiece, *The Search for the Ultimate Sink.*[41] Histories of environmental issues in individual cities are plentiful gems of environmental history, and among them are two fine pieces: Mike Davis' book on Los Angeles, *The Ecology of Fear*, and Ari Kelman on politics and infrastructure in New Orleans, *A River and Its City.*[42]

Environmental justice is inevitably associated with urban environmental history because historically populations of minorities and the poor have tended to concentrate in urban neighborhoods, but there are unfortunately abundant examples of environmental injustice in rural districts as well. The siting of polluting or otherwise dangerous facilities near people who lack the financial or political resources to fight such decisions is a concern of some environmental historians. Martin Melosi surveyed this aspect of environmental history in "Equity, Eco-Racism, and the Environmental Justice Movement."[43] An excellent collection of articles on the same subject is *Unequal Protection*, edited by Robert D. Bullard.[44]

The historical role of women in relationship to the environment has been an important theme in the writing of

9. View of suburbs of Las Vegas, Nevada, USA, from the air. The rapid spread of suburbia is a prominent aspect of contemporary environmental history.
Photograph taken by the author in 2000.

environmental history since its birth. This includes studies of women as leaders of the environmental movement, histories of ecofeminist philosophy, and analyses of feminine metaphors such as Mother Earth and Gaia in the conceptualization of the environment. Among the ideas explored include the notion that women are closer to nature than men, and that men have pursued the domination both of nature and of women in analogous ways. All these approaches are examined, for example, by Carolyn Merchant in her book, *Earthcare: Women and the Environment.*[45] Susan Schrepfer's *Nature's Altars* relates gender to environmentalism in terms of the appreciation of mountains and the aesthetic of the romantic sublime, and Jennifer Price discusses women's opposition to bird-feather hats in the early twentieth century, among many other comments, often tongue-in-cheek, on gender-related environmental attitudes.[46] Elizabeth D. Blum has written a historiographical essay on the whole subject, "Linking American Women's History and Environmental History: A Preliminary Historiography."[47]

Collaborators with Environmental History

Some historical subdisciplines that are more or less closely allied with environmental history had independent origins earlier than environmental history, and have recognized their affinity in the past two or three decades. Among these are the history of technology, agricultural history, and forest history. From the standpoint of environmental history, these subjects might be regarded as parts of its inquiry, since they investigate human interactions with the natural environment. Historians of technology and environmental historians now meet and hold sessions at one another's conferences. Agricultural history maintains a more autonomous identity, but scholars of either discipline sometimes write papers that are delivered at the other's meetings and are published in the corresponding journals. The relationship between forest history and environmental history is the closest; their societies in the US have considerable overlaps in membership and leadership and now share a common journal.[48]

Technology is an indispensable aspect of environmental history because it may be said that most major effects of humankind on the natural environment are accomplished through some form of technology. Indeed, it is technology in the broadest sense that has made possible the role of the human species as the active and ubiquitous disturber of ecosystems everywhere. One of the factors that have made environmental change increasingly widespread and rapid in the past two centuries is the advance in powerful technologies. A comprehensive guide to historical writing in the domain where technology and the environment overlap is "At the Intersection of Histories" by Jeffrey K. Stine and Joel A. Tarr.[49] It is, however, mainly limited to US scholarship. A history of technology that explores the environmental aspects of the subject is Carroll Pursell's *The Machine in America*.[50] The interplay of technology and urban environment is considered in a number of studies, notably those of Martin Melosi.[51] Water engineering and mining history are relevant subcategories.

The Society for the History of Technology (SHOT) was founded in 1958 to further the study of the past development of technology and its relationship to society and culture. Many otherwise well-researched studies of the history of technology failed to take account of environmental effects, even such an obvious one as pollution. A number of historians of technology began to recognize this as an unfortunate methodological lacuna, however, and found that they had a common interest with some environmental historians. *Environmental History Review*, the journal of the American Society for Environmental History (ASEH), published a special issue on "Technology, Pollution, and the Environment" in 1994. Members of SHOT formed a special interest group called "Envirotech," which holds sessions at the SHOT and ASEH meetings, and began publishing an Internet newsletter in 2001.[52]

Agricultural history would seem to occupy a place close to the center of gravity of environmental history from near the beginning, since humanity has been practicing agriculture for more than ten thousand years, and for at least the latter half of that period agriculture has provided the vast preponderance of the food that humans have drawn from nature. The alternative, that is, the uses of wild animals and plants, is relatively minor. Hunting supplies a minuscule proportion of protein needs for most of the world, and fishing, though of continuing importance, is partially giving way to forms of marine farming.

Agricultural history provided an impetus to the conception of environmental history both on the world scene and in North America, as Alfred W. Crosby pointed out.[53] Observers of environmental change as the result of agricultural encroachments included Pierre Poivre, Alexander von Humboldt, George Perkins Marsh, and James C. Malin, mentioned previously. Donald Worster, early in the formation of the field of environmental history, urged the writing of environmental history from an agrarian perspective.[54] An article tracing this strand was provided by Mart Stewart.[55] Many articles appearing in environmental history journals have agricultural history themes.

The Agricultural History Society was founded in 1919, and its journal, *Agricultural History*, has been published since 1926, and has included a number of articles with environmental history themes. The society's announced purpose includes facilitating research and publications on Rural Societies (the capitalization occurs in the Society's website). This indicates a concentration on social history, although a reading of the journal's table of contents indicates a parallel emphasis on economic history. Agricultural historians have demonstrated a recent and growing interest in the idea of sustainable agriculture, which some have associated with the term "agroecology" and with the examination of ecosystemic concepts and methods in agriculture.

"Just as people have biographies, so forests have their own histories that can be unraveled and documented," notes Michael Williams in his monumental world forest history, *Deforesting the Earth*.[56] Forest history is an older endeavor than environmental history in Europe, the US, and elsewhere, particularly in India. Much of the interest in forest history was generated by leaders of forest industries, managers, and foresters who saw their own activities in exploiting and manufacturing forest products as worthy of recording and commemoration. In the US, for example, the Forest History Society (FHS) traces its origin to the Forest Products History Association, formed within the Minnesota Historical Society in 1946. The FHS had an independent existence from 1959 with successive homes at Yale University and the University of California at Santa Cruz before arriving at its present location near Duke University in Durham, North Carolina, in 1984.[57] Along with a journal and a vigorous publishing program, the FHS has developed the world's most complete library and archive devoted to forest and conservation history, and also to environmental history, including databases and oral history. In 1996, the FHS entered into a partnership with ASEH, and both share in the publication of a journal, *Environmental History*. The literature on forest history, particularly in the US, is vast. For an overview, in addition to Williams' book mentioned earlier, one could consult his *Americans and Their Forests*, and the volume *This Well-Wooded Land* edited by Thomas R. Cox, Robert S. Maxwell, and Philip D. Thomas.[58] Harold K. Steen also has a more specialized book on forest and wildlife science.[59]

The fact that US environmental historians have played a prominent role in the emergence of environmental history as a historical subdiscipline in the last quarter of the twentieth century cannot be denied, but it has perhaps been overemphasized by some of its practitioners. Richard Grove, a British scholar of European imperialism in South Asia and Africa, is adeptly critical of a tendency of American environmental historians to be narrow or even isolationist, basing their analyses on American sources and rarely looking beyond the Atlantic, the Rio Grande, or even the Canadian border. Grove rightly points out that many of the major questions that occupy environmental historians had already been raised by historical geographers in the nineteenth and early twentieth centuries, many of them Europeans, and that American developments had significant parallels elsewhere. He does not dismiss American environmental scholars, but points out that many of the most significant of them were geographers such as Ellsworth Huntington, Ellen Churchill Semple, Carl Ortwin Sauer, and Clarence Glacken, the last-named an intellectual historian who wrote well before the 1960s in the years before the term "environmental history" had been used in its present meaning. In the earlier years of their subdiscipline, US environmental historians often rightly harked back to George Perkins Marsh as their predecessor and morning star, but tended to forget that his work, *Man and Nature*, starts with the Roman Empire and ranges widely over Europe and the Mediterranean as well as the US, and that his appreciation of environmental change caused by humans was matched by Alexander Humboldt, the British economist John Stuart Mill, and the imperial scientists Hugh Cleghorn and John Croumbie Brown.[60] By the turn of the twenty-first century, the isolationism of the American contingent in environmental history had yielded, though has perhaps not completely disappeared. A large number of American scholars, after all, work in global or non-American specialties, and those whose specialties remain in the US have been aware of comparative themes. A notable example of a work placing US environmental history in comparative context is Thomas R. Dunlap's *Nature and the English Diaspora*.[61] Marcus Hall does an interesting job of comparing environmental restoration in Italy and the US.[62] Also the organization of a European society, and of conferences across the globe, has encouraged the participation of American environmental historians and involved them in conversations with their counterparts elsewhere, as will be further noted in the following chapter.

4

Local, Regional, and National Environmental Histories

Introduction

The literature of regional, national, and local environmental histories outside the United States is now extensive.[1] Such studies constitute the foundation for accurate world environmental history in the future. The global must be based firmly on the local. Some of this work is being done by scholars working on their localities, nations, and regions. There is a growing international coterie researching the environmental history of their own lands in Australia, Austria, Brazil, Canada, Cuba, Finland, France, Germany, India, Italy, the Netherlands, New Zealand, Portugal, Russia, South Africa, Spain, Sweden, and Switzerland. It is to be expected that other nations will be added to this list. In many cases also, scholars work on areas of the Earth other than their own. This is particularly true of North Americans, Australians, or Europeans working on other parts of the world, such as the important studies by Dutch environmental historians of Indonesia, which result from personal connections and materials originating from the former colonial relationship.[2] One who has covered both home and abroad is Tim Flannery, an Australian scholar who taught Australian history as a visiting professor at Harvard, and not only wrote *The Future Eaters*,[3] an environmental history of Australasia, but also *The Eternal Frontier: An Ecological History of North America and Its Peoples.*[4]

An outstanding example of a study of one region that should be taken seriously by all writers on the world environment is *This Fissured Land: An Ecological History of India* by Madhav Gadgil and Ramachandra Guha.[5] The authors set their study of the South Asian subcontinent within a compelling philosophy of world environmental history extending from prehistory to the industrial age.

At the first formal conference of the American Society for Environmental History, held at the University of California at Irvine in January 1982, Donald Worster gave a banquet talk entitled "World Without Borders: The Internationalizing of Environmental History," later published in *Environmental Review* (now *Environmental History*).[6] In it, he called for a "postnationalist synthesis" that would take account of predicaments forced on historians by several transitions in modern culture away from the "vernacular" and local to the professional and global.

In the years after that talk was given, environmental historians evidently have taken Worster's words to heart. Even while he was speaking, many of them were moving in the international direction, while the subdiscipline maintained a strong core of work on American subjects that had characterized it from the beginning. The proceedings volume of the 1982 conference contained 26 articles, ten of which were on worldwide or non-US themes, four by non-US scholars.[7] A special international issue of *Environmental Review* in 1984 included five articles representing work on five continents.[8] Other periodicals that often opened their pages to articles on supra-national environmental history include *Environment and History*; *Capitalism, Nature, Socialism*; *Écologie Politique*; *Journal of World History*; and the *Pacific Historical Review*. The profession itself has now spread virtually worldwide. In discussing other nations where environmental historians had an established tradition, Worster cited only France and Britain. Today a speaker on the same subject might include several other European nations (Germany, Austria, Switzerland, the Netherlands, Belgium, Sweden, Denmark, Finland, the Czech Republic, Italy, Spain, Portugal, Greece, Russia, etc.), India, Canada, and

Australia. Latin America has a vigorous and growing group of environmental historians, notably in Brazil and Cuba. South Africa can also be added to the list.

Canada

Canadian scholarship in environmental history demands consideration separately from that in its southern neighbor, the US. Granted, there is abundant interchange between environmental historians in the two North American nations, attendance at one another's meetings, and, as of this writing, the American Society for Environmental History has met once in Canada, at Victoria, British Columbia. However, Canadians have their own distinct perspectives on many environmental subjects, not least because of their historical connections to the British Empire and the Commonwealth, and the unique presence of Francophone Quebec. The Briton Peter Coates maintains that the difference between Canada and the US reflects the overabundance of wilderness in the northern nation, and therefore the lower appeal of wilderness preservation there.[9] Graeme Wynn and Matthew Evenden of the University of British Columbia recently presented a topical analysis of recent Canadian environmental historiography, and the comments that follow are indebted to their study.[10] Wynn guest edited a special issue of *BC Studies*, "On the Environment," in 2004.[11]

The environmental history of American Indians, often referred to as First Nations in Canada, and the effects of European contact and colonialism, including epidemic disease, are represented by the works of Theodore Binnema, Douglas Harris, Arthur Ray, Jody Decker, Mary-Ellen Kelm, and others.[12] Another major theme is settlement with attendant resource development and environmental change, including regional studies by Neil Forkey, Matthew Hatvany, and Clint Evans,[13] and analyses of the relationship between development and social conflict by Richard Rajala, Jean Manore, and Matthew Evenden.[14]

As in the US, wilderness and wildlife have been dominant themes in Canadian environmental history writing, exemplified by Tina Loo and John Sandlos, while Kurkpatrick Dorsey has produced a study of treaties between the two nations on wildlife.[15] The history of science bearing on the environment, particularly the history of ecology, has been explored by Suzanne Zeller and Stephen Bocking, and Stéphane Castonguay wrote an important history of economic entomology.[16]

That the last-named work is in French is significant. French-speaking environmental historians in Quebec have held conferences on the subject, and there is a growing literature, among which might be mentioned Michelle Dagenais' article on recreation and cottage life on the outskirts of Montreal.[17]

Urban environmental history in Canada has been the subject of relatively few studies. Stephen Bocking guest edited a special number of *Urban History Review* on "The Nature of Cities" in 2005, treating a variety of problems and approaches.[18] Industrial blight as demonstrating environmental injustice in a waterfront district was investigated by Ken Cruikshank and Nancy Bouchier.[19]

The social construction of gender and nature as interrelated problems has been addressed by Cate Sandilands and Tina Loo. The latter investigates gendered aspects of big game hunting.[20]

Work in Canada has not been limited to writing on Canadian history, of course; Richard Hoffmann is one of the world's leading scholars on medieval European environmental history, to give one example.[21]

Europe

A brief look at writing in the environmental history of major regions outside North America may well begin with Europe. Although European writers entered the field perhaps even earlier than their North American counterparts, an organized and self-conscious body of environmental historians was later in forming. The journal *Environment and History* began publication in 1995 in the United Kingdom, with Richard Grove as editor. Although a European journal, it was by no means limited to research on European subjects; indeed, the first issue included articles on China, Africa, and Southeast Asia. The European Society for Environmental History (ESEH) was founded in 1999 and held its first conference in St Andrews, Scotland, in 2001. ESEH has regional sections that provide connections for environmental historians in every part of the continent including Russia. Ernst-Eberhard Manski, of Stevoort, the Netherlands, began a multilingual bibliographical database of European environmental history, and the effort continues under the aegis of ESEH.

A fine introduction to recent work in environmental history in Europe may be found in an article, "Environmental History in Europe from 1994 to 2004," edited by Verena Winiwarter.[22] It contains case studies by 13 authors highlighting significant work in most of the major countries. An earlier article (2000) by Mark Cioc, Björn-Ola Linnér, and Matt Osborn concentrates on the writing of environmental history in Northern Europe.[23]

The vigor and range of European environmental history may be sensed in *Dealing with Diversity*, the proceedings volume of the second ESEH conference in Prague, the Czech Republic, in 2003, and *History and Sustainability*, the proceedings of the third conference in Florence, Italy, in 2005, which together contain more than 140 brief versions of papers by as many authors, most of them Europeans.[24] A general impression one gains from these collections is that European environmental historians tend to use approaches derived from the sciences to a greater degree than their North American colleagues. An earlier excellent collection of essays in European environmental history is *The Silent Countdown*, edited by Peter Brimblecombe (UK) and Christian Pfister (Switzerland).[25] The Finnish editors Timo Myllyntaus and Mikko Saikku published a collection entitled *Encountering the Past in Nature*.[26]

A brief overview of British writing on environmental history may be found in "Sowing the Field of British Environmental History" by Matt Osborn.[27] Britain has a well-established tradition of writing on changes in the landscape as a result of human actions, and historical geographers there have often produced studies that are well within a definition of environmental history, although some of them, such as W. G. Hoskins' *The Making of the English Landscape*,[28] were written before environmental history was a recognized field. An influential book by H. C. Darby is *A New Historical Geography of England*, written in 1973.[29] I. G. Simmons, a geographer, is a very active environmental historian who has written on Britain,[30] the world, and the theory of environmental history. Environmental attitudes and philosophy in Britain in early modern times, a period that has not been studied to the extent it deserves, are analyzed by Keith Thomas.[31] Another recent study, limited to the last century, is John Sheail's *An Environmental History of Twentieth-Century Britain*.[32] Landscape history is very much alive in the work of Oliver Rackham, who has described the history of the British countryside with painstaking attention to the principles of ecological science in a number of well-illustrated books.[33] Pollution from burgeoning industry and the attempts to counteract it are traced in B. W. Clapp, *An Environmental History of Britain since the Industrial Revolution*,[34] and in Peter Brimblecombe's engaging study, *The Big Smoke*.[35] Brimblecombe is concerned with air pollution, while Dale H. Porter treats water pollution, sewage, odor, and the channelization of London's river in *The Thames Embankment*.[36]

Scotland has provided particularly fertile ground for environmental historians. Among them is the distinguished historian T. C. Smout, who has written and edited several books on the northern reaches of Britain, notably *Nature Contested* and *People and Woods in Scotland*.[37] Fiona Watson has written studies of the history of Scotland that are illuminated by her insights into environmental history, including *Scotland: From Prehistory to Present*.[38] Watson and Smout collaborated with Alan MacDonald on *A History of the Native Woodlands of Scotland, 1520–1920*.[39] Smout was one of the moving spirits in the Institute for Environmental History at the University of St Andrews in Scotland.

France has produced less environmental history in recent times than would be expected from the nation that gave birth to Pierre Poivre, and later Lucien Febvre, Fernand Braudel, Emmanuel Le Roy Ladurie and other great writers of the *Annales* School. Indeed, in the course of the latest decades the famous journal *Annales* itself has published a special issue on environment and history[40] but few other articles touching on the field. French historians of science have done excellent work on the history of ecology; among noted scholars are Pascal Acot and J. M. Drouin.[41] Acot has also written extensively on the history of climate and environmental philosophy.

Françoise d'Eaubonne launched the term "ecofeminism," with worldwide repercussions, in her book, *Le féminisme ou la mort* (*Feminism or Death!*) in 1974.[42] On the state and public history there are studies by Joseph Szarka and Emile Leynaud,[43] The literature on forest history is extensive, as would be expected of the nation where the study of forestry began. One can also mention the authors Andrée Corvol, and Louis Badré.[44] Among studies of the modern French environment are *Les français dans leur environnement* (*The French and their Environment*) by R. Neboit-Guilhot and L. Davy,[45] and *The Light-Green Society* by Michael Bess.[46] Geneviève Massard-Guilbaud, Christoph Bernhardt, and others have organized conferences and published proceedings on urban environmental history.[47]

The German-speaking portion of Europe includes Germany, Austria, and Switzerland, and environmental history has made great strides there in the past two decades. Verena Winiwarter (Vienna) has written *Umweltgeschichte: Eine Einführung* (*Environmental History: An Introduction*),[48] which does well in German what this book attempts in English. Christian Pfister (Bern) continues to make important advances in reconstructing past climates in western Europe.[49] A most notable contemporary author is Joachim Radkau, whose major book, *Natur und Macht* (*Nature and Power*),[50] will be considered in the next chapter. He has also written extensively on technology, economics, and politics. With Frank Uekötter, he wrote on the question of the role of environmentalism in the Nazi regime.[51] Several authors, including Anna Bramwell,[52] have connected conservation with fascism. The Nazi regime used propaganda linking nature with nationalism, but as Mark Cioc observes in a recent article, "In reality . . . the Nazis were committed to breakneck economic recovery and military expansion, not nature protection, and their twelve-year reign of terror

[1933–45] left a legacy of air and water pollution of breathtaking proportions," to say the least.[53] Cioc has written a significant study of the environmental history of the river Rhine.[54] On postwar environmentalism, Raymond Dominick wrote *The Environmental Movement in Germany*,[55] and there have been several studies of Die Grünen (the Green Party) including Klein and Falter, *Der lange Weg der Grünen* (*The Long Path of the Greens*).[56] The Green Movement affected politics in most Western European nations, but reached its apogee in Germany.

The environmental historians of the Netherlands and Belgium have produced several important studies, including G. P. van de Ven's collection, *Man-made Lowlands*,[57] covering the history of land reclamation, and a history of the conservation movement by H. J. van der Windt.[58] The *Yearbook for Ecological History* is published in Dutch.[59] Granted the location of the lowlands and the historical concern with water management, as in the expression "Holland against the Sea," it is not surprising that a number of environmental historians who write on the region are concerned with water history. Among them is Petra J. E. M. van Dam, who has written on the early modern Rhineland.[60] Also on the earlier period is William TeBrake's *Medieval Frontier: Culture and Ecology in Rijnland*.[61] In a somewhat wider geographic frame, Andrew Jamison and others compiled a comparative study of environmental movements in Sweden, Denmark, and the Netherlands, *The Making of the New Environmental Consciousness*.[62]

Scandinavia (Finland, Sweden and Denmark) is the scene of rapidly growing activity in environmental history. Its historiography in Finland is the subject of an informative article in English by Timo Myllyntaus, "Writing about the Past with Green Ink."[63] The Finnish term for environmental history is *ympäristöhistoria*, which was coined in the 1970s, but Myllyntaus traces its antecedents to earlier national landscape studies and to an "instinctive environmental consciousness." Environmental research there has centered on climate, forests, water resources, and landscape. Two major environmental history conferences with international participation have been held: at Lammi in the Lake District in 1992 and at Turku in 2005. Yrjö Haila and Richard Levins wrote on ecology, science, and society.[64] Jussi Raumolin has several publications on forest and mining history and technology, and the historical process of integration into the European economy.[65] On water conservation history, Simo Laakkonen did a study, *The Origins of Water Protection in Helsinki, 1878–1928.*[66]

Sweden has a vigorous scholarly community in environmental history, with several centers: the Department of Environmental History at Umeå University, the Center for Environment and Development Studies at Uppsala University, and the Human Ecology Division at Lund University. One of the leading scholars is Sverker Sörlin, who with L. Anders Sandberg edited a collection, *Sustainability, the Challenge.*[67] Anders Öckerman heads the program at Uppsala, and with Sörlin wrote a global environmental history that will be mentioned in the next chapter.[68] *The Danish Revolution, 1500–1800: An Ecohistorical Interpretation* by Thorkild Kjærgaard is a study of the early modern period.[69]

Environmental history appeared as such in the Czech Republic only in the late 1980s, but has made great strides in part as a result of the stimulus of the historical geographer, Leoš Jeleček of Charles University in Prague. As noted above, the second conference of ESEH was held in Prague in 2003. The proceedings of that conference contain a number of interesting papers by Czech and Slovak writers.[70] Work in the Czech Republic has included such lines of inquiry as long-term studies of land use and land cover changes, and historical climatology.

As in other European countries, environmental history in Hungary emerged with the background of historical geography. The relaxing of political supervision of scholarly work with the advent of the 1990s served as a welcome stimulus. Environmental history courses are now offered in Hungarian universities. A notable study is Lajos Rácz, *Climate History of Hungary Since the 16th Century.*[71] A series of important articles appeared in the volume, *People and Nature in Historical Perspective*, edited by Jószef Laszlovszky and Peter Szabó.[72]

The environmental history of Russia is the concern of several scholars at the Institute for the History of Science and Technology of the Russian Academy of Sciences, including Yuri Chaikovsky, Anton Struchkov, and Galina Krivosheina.

Douglas Weiner is the leading American scholar of Russia and the Soviet Union, and has produced several studies of Russian environmentalism, notably *Models of Nature*,[73] which analyzes conservation during the early Soviet period, and *A Little Corner of Freedom*,[74] which shows that environmental organizations in the Soviet Union provided an umbrella for scientists and critics. Weiner's article, "Russia and the Soviet Union," in the *Encyclopedia of World Environmental History*, provides a useful bibliography.[75]

The Mediterranean

The Mediterranean is a unique ecological region with the central sea as its unifying feature. The northern Mediterranean countries are, of course, part of Europe and could have been considered with equal rationale in the foregoing section. The environmental history of the Mediterranean as a whole has been well treated in John McNeill's *The Mountains of the Mediterranean World*,[76] which covers five representative localities and their peoples. J. Donald Hughes recently published *The Mediterranean: An Environmental History*,[77] with a chronological sweep from the first human inhabitants to the present, and offering case studies on Mesopotamia, the Roman Empire, and the dams on the Nile River at Aswan. *The Nature of Mediterranean Europe* by A. T. Grove and Oliver Rackham[78] is a well-illustrated survey of environmental processes rather than a history, and is marred by a quixotic attempt to prove that humans have not had any negative effect on the environment, particularly by causing deforestation, erosion, and desertification, from the end of the Bronze Age to the mid-twentieth century. Peregrine Horden and Nicholas Purcell have written *The Corrupting Sea*,[79] which contains interesting reflections on the idea of the Mediterranean, and exemplifies philosophy as much as history. The ancient Mediterranean world is discussed by J. Donald Hughes in *Pan's Travail: Environmental Problems of the Ancient Greeks and Romans*.[80]

The rise of environmental history in Spain and Portugal in the early 1990s was associated with increasing environmental concern and the interest of historians in the relevance of the methods of the natural and social sciences to their work. Among a coterie of these scholars are Manuel Gonzáles de Molina and J. Martínez-Alier, who edited a collection entitled *Naturaleza Transformada: Estudios de Historia Ambiental en España* (*Nature Transformed: Studies in Environmental History in Spain*).[81] Of particular interest to Spanish environmental historians has been the state of Spanish agriculture related to environmental constraints such as desertification. For example, there is "The Man-Made Desert," an article by Juan García Latorre, Andrés Sánchez Picón, and Jesús García Latorre.[82] Notable attention to work in environmental history has been evinced by CEHA, the Center for Studies of the History of the Atlantic, in Portugal on the island of Madeira. Alberto Vieira, of the Center, organized a conference in 1999 with scholars from Europe, the US, and Latin America, producing a volume, *História e Meio-Ambiente: O Impacto da Expansão Europeia* (*History and Environment: The Impact of the European Expansion*).[83] Unfortunately, it is not available in English.

Italy was the first Mediterranean country to have an active group of environmental historians, mainly scholars who moved in from closely related fields. Mauro Agnoletti was, and continues to be, a leading forest historian. He was the organizer of the third ESEH conference in Florence, 2005. Coming from agricultural history, Piero Bevilacqua is concerned about food supply crises such as BSE (mad cow disease), and has written *La mucca è savia* (*The Savvy Cow*).[84] His *Tra natura e storia* (*Between Nature and History*)[85] offered a step between agricultural history and environmental history.

The environmental history community in Greece is in the process of formation as of this date of writing. A conference, "The Environment in Greece: Historical Dimensions," held in Athens, used Greek as the conference language. The conference is organized by Chloe A. Vlassopoulou, who presented a paper on automobile pollution at the ESEH conference in Florence, 2005.[86] At the Prague 2003 conference, papers were presented by Alexis Franghiadis on the history of the Greek National Estates, which were virtual common lands open to the peasantry, and by

Alexandra Yerolympos on fire prevention in Mediterranean cities.[87]

Alon Tal is a lawyer rather than a historian, but his book, *Pollution in a Promised Land*, is, as the subtitle indicates, truly a competent environmental history of Israel.[88] It treats the whole variety of environmental problems in Israel, and avoids tendentious praise or pessimism.

India, South and Southeast Asia

South Asia has a strong tradition of academic history, and environmental history there is allied with ecology and history of science. The number, quality, and productivity of environmental historians in India are truly impressive. There, due to the historical experience of the subcontinent, particularly during the period of British rule, environmental history emphasizes forest history. Two leading researchers, Ramachandra Guha of the Nehru Memorial Museum and Library in New Delhi, and Madhav Gadgil of the Indian Institute of Science, Bangalore, coauthored *This Fissured Land*, an ecological history of India, mentioned above.[89] David Arnold and Ramachandra Guha edited a series of essays, *Nature, Culture, Imperialism*.[90] The History of Science division of NISTADS, the National Institute of Science, Technology, and Development Studies, New Delhi sponsored an impressive series of publications and conferences, with a Foreword by the distinguished historian of science, Deepak Kumar (Jawaharlal Nehru University) and Satpal Sangwan. A collection of important papers appeared as *Nature and the Orient*, edited by Richard Grove, Vinita Damodaran, and Satpal Sangwan.[91] Ajay Rawat of Kumaon University, Nainital, chronicled the deforestation of the Himalaya and its effect upon local people, especially women and tribal people, and has edited valuable collections on the history of forestry.[92] Ravi Rajan has written a book on forestry during the British imperial period.[93] Rana P. B. Singh of the National Geographical Society of India is a historical geographer who specializes in landscape and sacred topography, particularly the area of Banaras, the most important pilgrimage center of

Hinduism.[94] Subash Chandran, an ecologist, has studied ancient sacred groves that survive today, protected by villagers.[95] These occurred throughout India, but Chandran's studies, some written with Madhav Gadgil, center on the Western Ghats mountain range. The interaction between cattle grazing, forestry, colonial masters, and local people in Central India in the nineteenth century is the subject of *Ecology, Colonialism, and Cattle*, an excellent historical study by Laxman D. Satya.[96]

The *Indonesian Environmental History Newsletter* was published in Leiden, the Netherlands, edited by David Henley for EDEN (Ecology, Demography and Economy in Nusantara), an international group of scholars, for about a decade, but unfortunately ceased publication in 2003. Peter Boomgaard, the chair of EDEN, is as of 2005 writing an environmental history of Southeast Asia for the ABC–CLIO series, "Nature and Human Societies." He is the author of *Frontiers of Fear: Tigers and People in the Malay World*,[97] and with Freek Colombijn and David Henley, editor of *Paper*

10. A Brahmin praying on the bank of the holy river Ganges in Benares, India. Reverence for aspects of nature is a salient feature of historic human relationship to the environment. Photograph taken by the author in 1992.

Landscapes: Explorations in the Environmental History of Indonesia.[98] Writing by Indonesians on the environmental history of the archipelago has made a very small but encouraging beginning.

East Asia

The best introduction to environmental history in China is a recent article by Bao Maohong with that very title,[99] including extensive references to works by Chinese scholars in Chinese. Among the subjects of investigation mentioned by Bao are environmental protection, water control, urban environmental history, climate, population, the history of famine, and forest history. The subdiscipline of environmental history emerged there only in the late 1990s and early twenty-first century. An international symposium on Environment and Society in Chinese History, organized by Wang Lihua, was held at Nankai University, Tianjin, in 2005, with plans for proceedings. Among valuable studies by scholars outside China, one can confidently consult Mark Elvin's *The Retreat of the Elephants: An Environmental History of China.*[100] He and Liu Tsui-jung also edited an excellent collection, *Sediments of Time.*[101] The environmental mistakes of the period after the 1949 Revolution are elucidated by Judith Shapiro in *Mao's War against Nature.*[102] Among studies of earlier periods, *Tigers, Rice, Silk, and Silt* by Robert Marks is an exemplary study of responses by the imperial government to food crises in South China,[103] and the brief survey, *China*, by Yi-Fu Tuan is still valuable.[104] "Ecological Crisis and Response in Ancient China" by Lester Bilsky, in his edited volume, makes observations on the Qin and other early dynasties.[105] Nature protection is covered in Chris Coggins, *The Tiger and the Pangolin.*[106]

Japan has a well-established tradition of historical writing, but as yet has done very little with environmental history. Among writers outside Japan, Conrad Totman has an environmental history approach in his *History of Japan*, which begins with the sentence, "From an ecological perspective, the history of Japan is particularly interesting," and his *The*

Green Archipelago, based on many Japanese sources, is a first-rate forest history. Also note Brett Walker's *The Conquest of Ainu Lands.*[107]

Australasia and the Pacific Islands

A well-written guide to the situation in Australia and New Zealand, with an excellent bibliography, is "Environmental History in Australasia," by Libby Robin and Tom Griffiths.[108] Don Garden recently provided a comprehensive survey in *Australia, New Zealand, and the Pacific: An Environmental History.* An earlier reflective discussion of the same subject is "Environmental History and the Challenges of Interdisciplinarity: An Antipodean Perspective" by the New Zealander Eric Pawson and the Australian Stephen Dovers.[109] The journal *Environment and History* has highlighted this region in publishing two special issues, one on Australia, edited by Richard Grove and John Dargavel, and one on New Zealand, edited by Tom Brooking and Eric Pawson.[110] A controversial book that endeavors to cover the environmental history of all Australasia, including New Guinea and New Caledonia as well as Australia and New Zealand, is Tim Flannery, *The Future Eaters.*[111] Flannery pursued the hypothesis that, as Robin and Griffiths put it, "Aborigines and Europeans are both future-eaters, both short-term, short-sighted exploiters of nature."[112] This is a point of contention among environmental historians, that is, whether native peoples had through trial and error achieved a stable relationship with local ecosystems, and therefore whether colonialism destroyed this balance. Australia and New Zealand are similar in that each represents an effort by Britain to establish an antipodean colony that would be an image of the mother country in society and agriculture, but they contrast with each other sharply in landscape, native biota, and pre-European inhabitants, so their environmental histories have usually been treated separately.

Anyone seeking to become familiar with Australian environmental history might well begin with two volumes edited by Stephen Dovers, *Australian Environmental History* and

Environmental History and Policy.[113] One of the first historians to take an ecological tack in the narrative was Geoffrey Bolton in *Spoils and Spoilers*, Australia's first environmental history textbook.[114] He begins with an examination of the Aboriginal use of fire, continues with the attitudes of settlers to the supposedly inexhaustible supply of trees, land, and game, and concludes with the growing impact of urban and rural activities and the growth of the conservation movement. It would be remiss to describe the origin of environmental history in Australia without mentioning the work of Eric Rolls, a farmer and consummate writer who has both a practical and insightful grasp of ecological processes, and has inspired many historians.[115] Likewise, one can hardly ignore the immense contribution of the historical geographer, J. M. Powell, whose extensive works include *A Historical Geography of Modern Australia.*[116] The forest historian John Dargavel produced a reliable study, *Fashioning Australia's Forests,*[117] served as president of the Australian Forest History Society, which has held a number of conferences on forest and environmental history, and edited a series of volumes of the proceedings entitled *Australia's Ever-Changing Forests.*[118] Another good example of forest history is Tom Griffiths, *Forests of Ash*, examining the demise of the giant Eucalyptus forests of the state of Victoria.[119] The American author Stephen Pyne has written an environmental history of fire in Australia, *Burning Bush,*[120] one of his series on fire in various parts of the Earth. Studies of the history of the Australian environmental movement have been written by Tim Bonyhady (*Places Worth Keeping*),[121] by Libby Robin,[122] and by Drew Hutton and Libby Connors.[123] The usefulness of art and literature to an understanding of environmental history is exemplified by Tim Bonyhady's *The Colonial Earth.*[124]

New Zealand environmental historians, a very productive group, are justified in pointing out that their islands are ecologically unique within Australasia, and equally so within Polynesia, the cultural setting of the Maori. One of the questions in New Zealand environmental history is the relative degree to which the primeval landscape was altered respectively by the Maori settlers and by the Pakeha (non-Maori colonists). *Environmental Histories of New Zealand*, edited by Eric Pawson and Tom Brooking in 2002, is a representative collection of 18 articles.[125] James Belich's major two-volume New Zealand history, *Making Peoples* and *Paradise Reforged*, integrates environmental history for the early Maori, but becomes a more traditional political and social history in the colonial period.[126] Michael King does a bit more with our subject in *The Penguin History of New Zealand*.[127] The anthropologist Helen Leach investigates the history of horticulture among the Maori as well as Pakeha, and further abroad including the Pacific islanders.[128] *Ngā Uruora*, by Geoff Park, studies the historical course of removal of the coastal lowland forests, assigning more responsibility for the destruction to the Pakeha rather than the Maori. Alfred W. Crosby included a notable case study on New Zealand in his *Ecological Imperialism*.[129]

The Pacific Ocean is the largest of the Earth's regions, but as yet the writing of its environmental history has only begun. The definitions of the region vary; if the nations of the Pacific

11. Sheep on the South Island, New Zealand. One of the greatest environmental changes in New Zealand has been the transformation of the landscape for raising sheep, which far outnumber the human inhabitants.
Photograph taken by the author in 2000.

Rim are included, it is truly vast. *Environmental History in the Pacific World*, edited by J. R. McNeill,[130] has articles on diverse Pacific-facing lands from California and Chile to China and Australia, as well as the islands in between. John Dargavel, the forest historian, has convened several conferences and edited the collection, *Changing Tropical Forests: His-torical Perspectives on Today's Challenges in Asia, Australasia and Oceania.*[131] But more strictly, the region might be defined as Oceania, the island world chiefly including Melanesia, Micronesia, and Polynesia. That does not eliminate confusion, since New Guinea is in Melanesia and New Zealand is in Polynesia, and both are in Australasia. On the environmental history of Oceania, a fine article to begin with is John McNeill, "Of Rats and Men."[132] Patrick V. Kirch and Terry L. Hunt edited *Historical Ecology in the Pacific Islands*, a predominantly anthropological collection that includes "The Environmental History of Oceanic Islands" by Kirch.[133] A recent contribution is Paul D'Arcy's *The People of*

12.   Represented by costumed dancers in Jimbaran, Bali, Indonesia, the Barong is a fiercely friendly animal spirit that symbolizes positive elements of the environment.
Photograph taken by the author in 1994.

the Sea: Environment, Identity, and History in Oceania.[134] Two islands, Easter Island (Rapa Nui) and Nauru, have become famous as cautionary tales in environmental history, the first for pre-European history, as an island that was totally deforested by its inhabitants, and the second for twentieth-century history, as it was largely consumed and left wasted by the phosphate industry. Many books on Easter Island have appeared, including a fine chapter in Jared Diamond's *Collapse*,[135] but the most accessible monograph is *The Enigmas of Easter Island* by John Flenley and Paul Bahn.[136] For Nauru, there is the well-researched and very readable *Paradise for Sale* by Carl N. McDaniel and John M. Gowdy.[137]

Africa

A guide to Sub-Saharan African environmental history written by one of its leading practitioners at present is "Africa: Histories, Ecologies and Societies" by South African Jane Carruthers.[138] Her article places environmental history within the framework of social history, emphasizing changes in societies. Due to the importance of wildlife preservation and the creation of game parks from the colonial period onward, historians in Africa have given much attention to questions concerning conservation. An important collection is *Conservation in Africa*, edited by David Anderson and Richard Grove.[139] Another good example is William Beinart's *The Rise of Conservation in South Africa*.[140] The idea that Africa's environmental history is written on its landscapes is the theme of James C. McCann's important book, *Green Land, Brown Land, Black Land: An Environmental History of Africa, 1800–1990*. McCann says, "A fundamental leitmotif in this book is the premise that Africa's landscapes are anthropogenic, that is the product of human action."[141] He indicates that European colonists tended to regard Africa as a wild Eden that was ruined by wasteful African practices, while environmental historians today are more likely to blame colonial misunderstanding and exploitation. An earlier writer who helped to pioneer this idea is Helge Kjejkshus, in *Ecology Control and Economic Development in East African*

13.   Giraffes among trees of the savannah in Amboseli National Park, Kenya. Environmental history in Africa has analyzed the process and rationale of wildlife reserves and conservation.
Photograph taken by the author in 1989.

History.[142] The tendency to think of conservation as a topic outside the political sphere is demolished by Carruthers in *The Kruger National Park*[143] and in Clark Gibson's "Killing Animals with Guns and Ballots."[144] The journal *Environmental History* produced a special issue, "Africa and Environmental History," in 1999, with articles on migration, population, colonial science, and soil erosion.[145] Farieda Khan has turned attention to the neglected topic of the role of South African Blacks in conservation history, particularly in soil conservation.[146] *Environment and History* published a special issue on Zimbabwe in 1995, with articles examining issues of conservation, water, the ivory trade, and land disputes.[147]

Latin America

While Latin Americans and their friends in Europe and North America lament the late start of environmental history in the

Spanish- and Portuguese-speaking realms of the New World, and its lack of institutional support, anyone observing the youth, vigor, and productivity of environmental historians there today would certainly sense that the situation is rapidly changing. Conferences on "Historia Ambiental de Latinoamérica" (The Environmental History of Latin America) were held in Chile in 2003, Cuba in 2004, and a third was scheduled for Seville, the launch-pad for Spanish colonization in America. The number and variety of presentations scheduled for these conferences certainly place them in the same league with those of the ESEH and even the ASEH. The Brazilian scholar Lise Sedrez has provided a marvelous service by creating a website giving a very full bibliography of Latin American Environmental History.[148] An excellent introduction to environmental history written in Latin America is a 2001 article by Guillermo Castro Herrera, "Environmental History (Made) in Latin America."[149] Castro is also the author of *Naturaleza y Sociedad en la Historia de América Latina (Nature and Society in the History of Latin America*),"[150] which won the 1994 Casa de las Américas Award in Havana, Cuba. Noting the close association of the vision of nature with the idea of self-determination for the Latin American countries in the writings of the Cuban philosopher-patriot José Martí, Castro offers him as a contrasting counterpart to Thoreau in stimulating and environmental political consciousness. Earlier treatments of the scene are Nicolo Gligo and Jorge Morello, "Notas sobre la historia ecológica de América Latina" ("Notes on the Ecological History of Latin America");[151] and Luis Vitale, *Hacia una Historia del Ambiente en América Latina (Toward a History of the Environment in Latin America).*[152] An anthology, *Estudios sobre Historia y Ambiente en América (Studies on History and Environment in America)*, edited by Bernardo García Martínez and Alba González Jácome,[153] was published in 1999 with the support of the Pan-American Institute of Geography and History of the Organization of American States. Environmental histories of Latin American nations include *Tierra Profanada: Historia Ambiental de México (A Profaned Land: An Environmental History of Mexico)* by Fernando Ortiz Monasterio, Isabel Fernández, Alicia Castillo, José Ortiz Monasterio, and Alfonso Bulle Goyri; and *Memoria*

Verde: Historia ecológica de la Argentina (*Green Memory: An Ecological History of Argentina*) by Antonio E. Brailovsky and Dina Foguelman.[154]

There is an important body of works in English on the environmental history of Latin America. Alfred Crosby's works, especially *The Columbian Exchange*,[155] have strongly influenced both North American and Latin American scholars with ideas related to the fact that European incursions into the New World were not merely military conquests, but biological transfers including invasive animals, plants, and microorganisms as well as human populations. Elinor Melville's *A Plague of Sheep* investigates environmental consequences of the conquest of Mexico, specifically the ecological degradation of the valley of Mezquital.[156] Warren Dean wrote *With Broadax and Firebrand: The Destruction of the Brazilian Atlantic Forest*,[157] a masterpiece of environmental history described in Chapter One. Dean's tragic death in Santiago in 1994 prevented the completion of a projected book on the Amazon rainforest, possibly a sequel to his *Brazil and the Struggle for Rubber*.[158]

The Ancient World and the Middle Ages

More work is needed in chronological periods that have been largely missing until recently. Generally speaking, this means anything before about 1800. The Middle Ages remained relatively untouched before it was opened up for environmental history by scholars such as Richard Hoffmann, William TeBrake, Petra van Dam, Charles R. Bowlus, Ronald E. Zupko, and Robert A. Laures.[159] The field of classical Mediterranean environmental history is inadequately covered, partly due to the conservatism of the academic fields of classics and ancient history, but the present author, J. Donald Hughes, has done some work on the subject,[160] and there is published writing of good quality by Russell Meiggs, Robert Sallares, Thomas W. Gallant, Günther E. Thüry, Helmut Bender, Karl-Wilhelm Weeber, and J. V. Thirgood.[161] Richard Hoffmann and Elinor G. K. Melville organized a conference on pre-industrial environmental history in Toronto, Canada, in April, 1996. A second conference on that theme would serve a very good purpose, and is overdue.

Conclusion

The spread of the international network of environmental historians has been rapid in some areas and slower in others. There are several factors responsible for this. One is the prior existence of contact between academic communities in history and historical geography. Another is the presence or absence of an active environmental movement embodying concern for the issues studied by environmental history. In addition, the openness of university and state structures to innovation has definitely been an influence.

While the antecedents of environmental history arose in Europe and the colonial realms of European powers, it is nonetheless true that the academic discipline of environmental history flourished first in the United States, and continues a predominance of numbers of scholars and publications there which has undoubtedly been both a positive and negative force. It is positive in the influence of leading scholars such as Donald Worster, Alfred Crosby, William Cronon, Carolyn Merchant, and others, whose work is almost universally cited by environmental historians across the globe. It has been negative in that environmental history is notably absent from nations that most adamantly reject US, or Western influences. This is not to say that environmental historians elsewhere are not sharply critical of the views of US environmental historians. For example, Indian scholars such as Ramachandra Guha have rejected what they see as a preoccupation with wilderness in the American environmental movement, and have emphasized the importance of local communities, which they see as lacking in American environmental history. Some American environmental historians have taken this to heart, and have produced histories that emphasize the role of indigenous peoples and ethnic groups. There is a concern everywhere to identify and define the factors that have operated in the environmental history of each region and country. The result is a series of insights in theory and method that are shaping environmental histories in various societies. These insights have reciprocally transformed environmental history in the US as well. It is to be hoped that viable communities of scholars in environmental history will yet appear in the great places of the Earth that still are missing them.

5

Global Environmental History

Introduction

The need to study environmental history on a planetary scale is self-evident. Environmental factors operated beyond single cultures and regions even in early times, with the spread of epidemics, the diffusion of agricultural innovations, and the movement of human populations. Global environmental change accelerated in the early modern period, with biological exchanges brought about by explorers, traders, and settlers. Environmental issues in the twentieth and early twenty-first centuries have increasingly assumed worldwide proportions. The atmosphere carries pollutants, radioactive particles, and volcanic dust from their sources across the continents, is the medium of catastrophic storms, and its chemical composition and rising temperature reflect the "greenhouse effect," a cause of global warming. The world's oceans make up seven-tenths of the Earth's surface, and affect not only the coastlands and islands, but the Earth as a whole by serving as an "ultimate sink,"[1] absorbing and emitting gases, including water vapor and carbon dioxide, and their temperature may ultimately have an even greater effect on global warming than that of the atmosphere. Human activities today are less often circumscribed by specific ecosystems (although even these cross national borders), and more often extend throughout the biosphere that transcends every national frontier. World trade has ensured that food energy produced by soils in one country may be consumed on a distant continent, and that the price of oil will have effects far from the sources of that resource. Distant demands have encouraged overfishing, and wild species have been reduced to near or total extinction. All these factors can be themes of environmental history, so it seems to follow that at least some environmental historians would take world history as their scale. But it is daunting. If the Earth is a small planet, it is still enormous when measured by the perceptions of its inhabitants, and in ecological terms, it is exceedingly varied. It is a challenge for any author to try to embrace it all or to say anything in general that is true of its diversity. Even so, a few have made an attempt at a synthesis.

Books on World Environmental History

World environmental history is, of course, the most widely embracing approach to the subject, and the one that potentially can erase the greatest number of borders and provide useful international comparisons. It is also one of the earliest kinds of environmental history to appear.

A cross-fertilization between history and the sciences, particularly ecology, produced abundant fruit in world environmental history. This was the thrust of an international symposium at Princeton chaired by Carl O. Sauer, Marston Bates, and Lewis Mumford in 1955. Its proceedings, entitled *Man's Role in Changing the Face of the Earth*, edited by William L. Thomas, Jr., was a seminal collection of essays spanning the planet and the chronological sweep of human history, and laid the foundation for later work bridging science and history. One example of this was William Russell's *Man, Nature, and History*.[2] Although somewhat elementary, it was almost alone as a college text in the field in 1969. The Thomas volume was emulated and in some ways surpassed by a 1990 collection, *The Earth as Transformed by Human Action: Global and Regional Changes in the*

Biosphere over the Past 300 Years, edited by B. L. Turner II, William C. Clark, Robert W. Kates, John F. Richards, Jessica T. Mathews, and William B. Meyer.[3] Although this collection was limited to the eighteenth through twentieth centuries, as its title suggests, it was authoritative and more systematic than the Thomas volume.

Alfred Crosby's earlier work, including his groundbreaking *The Columbian Exchange*,[4] combined medical and ecological science and history to demonstrate the biological impact of the Europeans and their domestic animals and plants, and the diseases to which they had developed resistance, on the Americas. He then expanded his purview, in *Ecological Imperialism*,[5] showing that the Europeans toted their "portmanteau biota" to temperate neo-Europes in many hitherto isolated lands, where they achieved demographic takeovers.

Until recently, attempts by historians to write environmental histories of the world have been few: not surprisingly, due to the relatively recent delineation of the field and the vastness of the subject. An early effort to write a global environmental history was Arnold Toynbee's *Mankind and Mother Earth*,[6] but it was unfinished at the time of the author's death, and suffers from several flaws, the most important of which is an extremely cursory treatment of modern history. Despite a promising title and a prefatory section that takes ecology seriously, it remains for the most part a conventional political-cultural narrative repeating observations made in his earlier works. It can be appreciated as a gesture, however. Late in life, Toynbee apparently recognized that his *Study of History*[7] had failed to give ecological process the role it demanded, and the later book might be viewed as an incomplete attempt to remedy that defect.

Ian Simmons, a geographer at Durham, wrote two books that take a schematic look at world environmental history, firmly based on scientific data. They are *Changing the Face of the Earth: Culture, Environment, History*, and *Environmental History: A Concise Introduction*.[8] Geography is a discipline whose scholars are perhaps less inclined than historians to hesitate in taking a global view when they look at history. Among other geographers who have done so are Andrew Goudie, in *The Human Impact on the Natural*

Environment,[9] and Annette Manion, in *Global Environmental Change: A Natural and Cultural History.*[10] The Australian, Stephen Boyden, wrote *Biohistory: The Interplay between Human Society and the Biosphere.*[11]

Jared Diamond, a master of several fields who also justifiably claims to be an environmental historian, and who is eclectic in his sources of evidence, has written *Guns, Germs, and Steel: The Fates of Human Societies,*[12] and *Collapse: How Societies Choose to Fail or Succeed,*[13] which treat the influence of geography and biology on history, and human cultural responses, from the earliest times in often arresting ways. They are also engagingly written and, uniquely for books in this field, both have spent many weeks in the newspaper best-seller lists. They are undoubtedly the environmental history books most widely read by the general public, and deserve attention for that reason as well as their intrinsic merits. In *Guns, Germs, and Steel,* Diamond asks why technologically advanced civilizations appeared in the places they did, among some societies and not among others. He rejects the idea that it might be because certain peoples are more intelligent and inventive than others, since average intelligence has been shown to be more or less the same across all human groups, racially speaking. The answer, then, must lie in differences of geography and environment. Among these differences are the availability or unavailability of domesticable plants and animals, and the orientation of arable continental lands on an east–west axis (offering domesticates the ability to spread to areas at similar latitudes), rather than a north–south axis. Many critics have regarded this line of argument as environmental determinism, but Diamond rejects that label. The mere presence of environmentally suitable locales does not mean that any people living there will develop an advanced technology. *Collapse* can be seen as a defense against the criticism of environmental determinism. In it, Diamond attempts to answer a question that is the converse of the one in *Guns, Germs, and Steel.* To paraphrase his subtitle, why do societies choose to fail or succeed? Examining the historical collapses of a number of societies, Diamond groups the reasons for collapse into five categories: climatic change, hostile neighbors, trade partners, environmental problems, and a society's response to environmental problems. It is in the last category that a society may "choose" to fail or succeed, and if it can choose, then its environment does not totally determine the outcome. Diamond provides illustrations of cases where two societies existed at the same time in much the same place, but one failed and the other succeeded (as exemplary pairs, the Norse and Inuit in Greenland, and Haiti and the Dominican Republic on Hispaniola). Another pair, however, Easter Island (Rapa Nui) and Tikopia, both Polynesian societies on Pacific islands, raises a further question. Easter Island was completely denuded of trees by its inhabitants and suffered a population collapse, but Tikopia has retained a stable population and is still tree-covered. Diamond and his colleague Barry Rolett identified nine environmental factors that affect the likelihood of deforestation on Pacific islands, and it appears that Tikopia does better than Easter Island on about five out of the nine. Easter Island is near the bottom on all nine, and if the environmental deck was stacked so severely against Easter Island, can it really be said that the Easter Islanders "chose" to fail? Well, the wealth and religion of the Tikopia were based on pigs, and they nevertheless chose to kill all the pigs because they were consuming the resources of the small island. The prestige and religion of the Easter Islanders were based on the erection of huge stone statues, and they kept putting them up until all the trees, whose trunks had been used to move them, were gone. Why did one people, and not the other, see the problem they had and act to alleviate it? Diamond speculates on possible answers, and gives plausible reasons. Although a definitive one may escape us, he should be thanked for investigating the question.

Also popular and widely available, Clive Ponting's *Green History of the World*,[14] a survey of environmental issues through history, begins with the problem of the destruction of the ecosystems of Easter Island as a parable for environmental history, and proceeds chronologically at first and then topically. Some teachers of environmental history who have used it with their students have found the organization confusing. Although Ponting touches on most of the salient themes and his broad knowledge is impressive, his style is journalistic and his documentation woefully inadequate in that there are no footnotes and only a brief "Guide to Further Reading" rather than endnotes or a bibliography.

14. Moai, statues of ancestral figures made of volcanic rock,
about 10 m (30 f) in height, at Ahu Tongariki, Easter Island
(Rapa Nui), Chile. Easter Island is one of the prime examples
of a society that depleted its own environment and suffered
a collapse.
Photograph taken by the author in 2002.

A very useful contribution is the writing of world environ-
mental histories by scholars in continental Europe and elsewhere, whose viewpoints offer challenging perspectives.
Scandinavian historians recently have made contributions
to the literature on world environmental history.[15] In 1998,
Sverker Sörlin and Anders Öckerman wrote a useful outline
of global environmental history, *Jorden en Ö: En Global
Miljöhistoria* (*Earth an Island: A Global Environmental
History*), primarily focused on the modern world.[16] Hilde
Ibsen used the "ecological footprint" concept to interpret the
history of ecological interactions between human societies
and their environments.[17]

Two global environmental histories appeared at the turn
of the twenty-first century. Joachim Radkau, a professor at
the University of Bielefeld in Germany, published *Natur und
Macht: Eine Weltgeschichte der Umwelt* (*Nature and Power:
A World History of the Environment*) in 2000,[18] which as

the title indicates, places environmental history in the context of themes to which the historical profession as a whole is accustomed. Including topics from prehistoric hunting groups to globalization and environmental security (or insecurity) in present world politics, it is remarkably well balanced both chronologically and geographically. Intelligently and trenchantly expressed in German, it will soon appear in an English translation.

Shortly after the publication of Radkau's book, a work appeared by J. Donald Hughes, the present author, entitled *An Environmental History of the World: Humankind's Changing Role in the Community of Life.*[19] My book offers a chronological sweep from prehistory to the contemporary. Each chapter consists of an introduction to a broad chronological period followed by case studies of selected periods and places. My approach emphasizes the mutual relationships between human societies and the ecosystems of which they are part, investigating the ways in which environmental changes, often the result of human actions, have caused historical trends in human societies. The chapters covering the twentieth century discuss the physical impact of the huge growth in population and technology, and the human responses to these trends. Moral obligations to nature and the conundrum of a sustainable balance between technology and the environment are also considered.

Sing C. Chew, a sociologist, has turned into a competent historian and written an environmental history of 5,000 years, from the appearance of the first cities to the present, *World Ecological Degradation.*[20] As the title indicates, this is what many environmental historians term a declensionist narrative. Chew states his thesis and follows it with admirable directness: urbanized societies have exploited and depleted the environment, everywhere and throughout history. The most powerful engines of destruction, he maintains, are accumulation, urbanization, and population growth. By accumulation, he designates the acquisition of wealth not simply in the form of financial capital, but all the material aspects of civilization, which are produced from the physical resources of the natural environment and inevitably exhaust them. Urbanization drives an intensive utilization of resources that transforms the landscape. Population growth exacerbates the first two phenomena and generates increasing stress on the environment. Among the processes of ecological degradation, Chew treats one in detail: deforestation. It is an excellent choice as an example, since it occurred from the discovery of fire to the present, and can be documented and measured. It stands as a proxy for other forms of degradation that accompany it, such as floods, erosion, habitat loss, and the deterioration of ecosystems. One of the most original elements in his analysis is the idea that "dark ages" are the result of expanding cultures exhausting the resources available to them. Though disasters for civilizations, these periods offer a measure of recovery to Nature. There have been individuals and groups that have objected to the trashing of the environment by societal elites. Why have these not had a greater effect in teaching humankind to avoid the "degradative encounters" that human communities experienced? Chew believes this is due in part to the domination of society by leading groups committed to "maximal utilization of resources for the most gains,"[21] and in part to human irrationality.

A number of collections of articles on world environmental history have appeared. The nature of the subject almost assures that authors from other disciplines will appear among the historians. This is true of Lester J. Bilsky's *Historical Ecology: Essays on Environment and Social Change* (1980),[22] which has pieces representing time frames from the prehistoric through modern, and to some extent of Donald Worster's *The Ends of the Earth* (1988).[23] This choice collection includes articles on population, the Industrial Revolution, India, Africa, the Soviet Union, and three on the US in addition to Worster's useful introduction and widely cited appendix, "Doing Environmental History."[24] J. Donald Hughes' collection, *The Face of the Earth: Environment and World History* (2000),[25] contains essays only by historians, including pieces on biodiversity, eco-racism in the US, the Pacific, Australia, Russia and India. Like Worster's edited volume, it is predominantly but not exclusively modern in scope.

Some studies have appeared that encompass world environmental history in a particular time period. The finest recent monograph in the field is a history of the last century by John R. McNeill: *Something New Under the Sun: An*

Environmental History of the Twentieth-Century World.[26]
It is the first synoptic world environmental history of the
twentieth century. McNeill traces the environmental and
related social changes, unique in scale and often in kind, that
characterize the period, and maintains that the twentieth
century was different in kind, not only in degree, from any of
the previous ones, in that "the human race, without intending
anything of the sort, has undertaken a gigantic uncontrolled
experiment on the earth."[27] Where a look at previous times is
necessary to understand the twentieth century, he succinctly
provides the background. He explains that contemporary
culture is adapted to abundant resources, fossil fuel energy,
and rapid economic growth, patterns that will not easily be
altered should circumstances change, and the behavior of
human economy in the twentieth century has increased the
inevitability of change. The engines of change are conversion
to a fossil fuel-based energy system, very rapid population
growth, and a widespread ideological commitment to economic growth and military power. McNeill includes a perceptive section on world economic integration. This book bids
fair to become a classic of environmental history.

Another study of the environmental history of a historical
period is by John F. Richards, with the title, *The Unending
Frontier: The Environmental History of the Early Modern
World,*[28] covering the period between the fifteenth and eighteenth centuries. As the title suggests, Richards emphasizes
frontiers as the places where environmental changes were
occurring most rapidly. The argument of the book is that
the salient patterns of the world were the expansion of
Europeans across much of the rest of the globe and progress
in human organization in Europe, India, and East Asia.
A chapter discusses the state of our knowledge of climatic
history; the Little Ice Age made its appearance during this
time and its effects cannot be ignored. Richards' treatment
is exemplary; he gives due importance to the geographical
setting, the biological factors, the indigenous peoples whom
he portrays neither as helpless victims nor as ecological
saints, and the adaptations of the Europeans and their
imported domestic animals, plants, and pathogens. The last
section, entitled "The World Hunt," gives an extraordinary
overview of the way in which Europeans ranged the world

in search of organic resources and, treating them as inexhaustible, managed to reduce the incredible abundance and diversity of wildlife at the beginning of the Early Modern Period to a waning remnant at the end. He notes the economic advantages derived from the hunt and the environmental changes produced by the removal of species. Richards gives attention to the areas where the action was happening, and that means the frontiers, which are his central theme. He has little to say about older theaters where development had already occurred, such as the Mediterranean basin and Near East, or the areas beyond the frontiers where the full modern encounter was yet to take place, namely Oceania, Africa north of the area around the Cape, and the North American west. This substantial volume can stand beside John McNeill's twentieth-century environmental history, *Something New Under the Sun*, as a complementary work. The two together almost cover the modern world; obviously what we need now is an environmental history of the nineteenth century to bridge the gap between them. Each of these authors notes that the world of the time he describes was unprecedented in terms of worldwide environmental changes caused by human economic activity, and both are right.

A new perspective on global environmental history is offered by Robert B. Marks in *The Origins of the Modern World*.[29] Spanning the early modern and modern worlds from 1400 to 1850, Marks reverses the usual perspective and steadfastly keeps China, instead of Europe, in the center. From this viewpoint, the "Rise of the West" was not inevitable or the result of Europe's inherent superiority, but "the story of how some states and peoples benefited from historically contingent events and geography to be able, at a certain point in time (a historical conjuncture), to dominate others and to accumulate wealth and power."[30]

Topics of Global Importance

Another category consists of studies and collections that are global in scope, but deal with special topics. These include books on world forest history, including the major recent monograph by Michael Williams, *Deforesting the Earth: From Prehistory to Global Crisis*,[31] an authoritative masterwork that relates the historical course of human impact on forests across the world's continents and islands. Williams has the knack of providing just the right specific details to bring the narrative to life. To give an example, he does not just say that the demand for fuel in the sugar industry caused deforestation in the West Indies in the seventeenth century, but reports a request from Barbados for coal from England to boil sugar because there were no trees on the island. Again, to illustrate the widespread publicizing in the US of tropical rainforest destruction, he recalls an electronic billboard above the Hard Rock Café in Beverly Hills, California, that kept pace with the decreasing rainforest area as it flashed the decline toward zero.[32] There are good collections on world forests, such as *Global Deforestation and the Nineteenth-Century World Economy*, edited by Richard P. Tucker and John F. Richards;[33] and *Tropical Deforestation: The Human Dimension*, edited by Leslie E. Sponsel, Thomas N. Headland, and Robert C. Bailey.[34]

On the history of fire, Stephen J. Pyne has given environmental historians a series of excellent books on fire in selected parts of the world, "Cycle of Fire," and an overview, *World Fire: The Culture of Fire on Earth*.[35] The latter book is more than a history of forest fires. It is a global history of human involvement with the element of fire in all its forms from its origin in geological epochs to the high-tech fire powering the information revolution and the world market economy. Pyne includes cities, where the built environment served as fuel, as in London in 1666 and San Francisco in 1906. He elucidates the technology of fire from charcoal in metallurgy to gunpowder, the steam engine, and fossil fuels in the twentieth century, including cookery, the fiery philosophy of Heraclitus, and the Kyoto Protocol, all in proper context, and concludes with a look at fire in the new millennium. Pyne's style is the essence of scholarly accessibility.

On climate, Richard Grove and John Chappell's intriguing book, *El Niño: History and Crisis*,[36] mentioned in chapter 1, investigates the worldwide effects on human history of oscillating oceanic currents and heightened temperatures usually called *El Niño* (and its cooler counterpart *La Niña*).

15.   A trained Asian elephant and a power line in north India,
        symbolizing two forms of energy typical of different periods
        in environmental history.
        Photograph taken by the author in 1994.

While *El Niño* proper is a phenomenon of the Pacific Ocean,
these authors indicate its connection with a world system
including periodic occurrences such as a similar oscillation
in the North Atlantic, and the South Asian monsoon. These
are examined as possibly contributing causes of historical
events such as economic crises brought about by food shortages, and the consequent fall of governments.

   A theme that falls within the area of global environmental
history is the study of the environmental impacts of imperialism. Alfred Crosby's deservedly much-noted *Ecological
Imperialism* was mentioned earlier in this chapter.[37] Another
landmark book is Richard Grove's *Green Imperialism*,

discussed in chapter 2,[38] which traces the origin of modern ecological thought, conservationism, and environmental history to a group of professionals, especially medical scientists and biologists, who were civil servants in the French, British, and Dutch maritime empires in the seventeenth and eighteenth centuries, and up to the late nineteenth century. Grove points out the particular importance of islands in the development of environmental thinking, since their small size meant that the impacts of human actions on the landscape became evident relatively rapidly. A book that traces much the same theme through the period 1895–1945, with emphasis on the fledgling science of ecology, is Peder Anker's *Imperial Ecology*.[39] Anker argues that ecology made rapid strides because imperial patrons wanted scientific tools to manage nature and native cultures in the British Empire. Richard Drayton's *Nature's Government*[40] also sees science as an instrument of imperialism and racism, in the British Empire to 1903, but providing a philosophical background going back through the Renaissance to Aristotle and Theophrastus in ancient Greece. Drayton emphasizes the role of botanical gardens, particularly the great Royal Botanic Gardens at Kew, in "improving" the world under Britain's aegis. A study of a related theme in India, a colonized world in itself, is Deepak Kumar's *Science and the Raj, 1857–1905*.[41] The important role of Scotland and Scots in the environmental story of the British Empire is explored by John MacKenzie, in *Empires of Nature and the Nature of Empires: Imperialism, Scotland and the Environment*.[42] A good collection of articles on imperialism and the environment is *Ecology and Empire: Environmental History of Settler Societies*, edited by Tom Griffiths and Libby Robin.[43]

The environmental effects of what many have called the American Empire extend far beyond areas directly administered by the US, of course. Richard Tucker takes on this subject in his careful, well-documented book, *Insatiable Appetite: The United States and the Ecological Degradation of the Tropical World*,[44] covering the period from the 1890s to the 1960s. Tucker portrays important ways in which American business and government have impacted the warmer regions of the globe. The book is organized by types of renewable biological resources that were exploited, with chapters devoted to sugar, bananas, coffee, rubber, beef, and timber. The geographic regions emphasized are Latin America; the Pacific islands including Hawai'i, the Philippines and Indonesia; and Liberia in West Africa. Tucker's intent is to describe the unsustainability of much of the development that occurred, and the biotic impoverishment including deforestation, loss of species, destabilization of soil and cropping systems, and other environmental damage that re-sulted, including its effects on people such as villagers and forest residents. The author's approach is balanced, but the overall picture is that of ecological disasters driven by exploitation.

Thomas Dunlap has taken an innovative approach in writing *Nature and the English Diaspora*,[45] the environmental history of what might be termed, in terms provided by Crosby, Britain and the "Neo-Britains": Canada, the US, Australia, and New Zealand. It is a comparative history of ideas about nature in these four English-speaking countries, from "native nature" through natural history, ecology, and environmentalism.

Environmental Movements

There are histories of the environmental movement around the world. Ramachandra Guha, in *Environmentalism: A Global History*,[46] offers an analysis of the shared aims and dissimilarities of environmental aims and activism in India, the US, Europe, Brazil, the Soviet Union, China, and other corners of the world. Guha's approach is historical, spanning the time from nationalistic ruralism to social ecology, from Virgil to the Nobel prizewinner Wangari Maathai. In recent years, the creation of the United Nations Environment Programme and other international agencies, both governmental and non-governmental, concerned with conservation and sustainable development, has opened a new field for historians. John McCormick wrote a book-length study, *Reclaiming Paradise: The Global Environmental Movement*,[47] emphasizing specifically international aspects of the environmental movement from the founding of the United Nations in 1945 through the Brundtland Commission Report of 1987. The idea that technological and financial fixes do not address the deeper changes called for by global environmental problems and ecological consciousness is the theme of Carolyn Merchant's *Radical Ecology: The Search for a Livable World*,[48] which has sections on deep ecology, social ecology, Green politics, and ecofeminism, and includes descriptions of modern activist movements such as Earth First!, Chipko, and indigenous rainforest action groups.

World History Texts

Environmental history has an increasingly prominent place in textbooks on world history. John McNeill asserts that the patterns of human environmental relations are the most important aspect of twentieth-century history,[49] and a case might be made that this was no less true of preceding centuries and millennia, even if awareness was lacking. Prior to the past decade, world history textbooks had given little attention to environmental issues except possibly in their chapters on prehistory and on the late twentieth century. But at the present time environmental historians increasingly are listed among the co-authors, and there is evidence that their perspectives are now reflected across the entire time frame of some (but not all) of these books that are so important to the undergraduate education of the student generation of the early twenty-first century. As a teacher of a world history course every year, I have not yet found a totally satisfactory text that I can wholeheartedly recommend, but have noticed an improvement in the past five years or so.[50]

The story line, or organizing principle, of virtually every world history textbook in recent times is "development." The word occurs everywhere, often in titles such as "The Development of Civilization."[51] The word is almost never defined, nor is the case for it as an organizing principle argued. It is simply accepted as an unquestioned good. The story as usually told takes humankind from one level of economic and social organization to the next in a nearly triumphal ascent. Even if "development" is not defined, it is clear that what is meant is economic growth driven by advances in technology. Although world history texts describe achievements in the arts and sciences, what they regard as the goal of development is obviously not finer literature than Homer's, paintings that outdo Lascaux, or even discoveries in physics that will surpass Einstein's. It is the creation of factories, energy facilities, financial institutions, and the ever-increasing use of the Earth's resources for human purposes. And as to the environment, the story of development for the most part ignores the living and non-living world. For a nation to succeed in development would be for its natural resources to be used, for its forests to be turned into lumber and its coal and iron ore deposits into steel. In the process, the air would become more polluted and the rivers would become more laden with the products of erosion and waste. There is a recognition on the part of environmentalists and developers alike that to protect the environment is to curb development, and to develop is typically, if perhaps not inevitably, to degrade the environment. Human beings seem to want both goods, while recognizing their prevailing incompatibility. The new narrative of world history must have ecological process as its major theme. It must keep human events within the context where they really happen, and that is the ecosphere. The story of world history, if it is to be balanced and accurate, will inevitably consider the natural environment and the myriad ways in which it has both affected and been affected by human activities. Ecological process is a dynamic concept. It implies that the interrelationship of humans and the natural environment undergoes continual changes, some positive and some destructive. These changes make environmental history just as necessary as ecological science in explaining the present predicament of humankind and nature.

Conclusion

Finally, world environmental historians in the future will find themselves increasingly challenged by the need to explain the background of the world market economy and its effects on the global environment. Supranational instrumentalities threaten to overpower conservation in a drive for what is called sustainable development, but which in fact envisions no limits to economic growth. There is a growing literature of criticism of this trend by environmental economists including Robert Costanza, Herman Daly, Hilary French, and James O'Connor,[52] which could inform historians whose field of inquiry is the international landscape as they take a long-needed, hard look at the impacts of the free trade regime on human societies and the biosphere. It is to be hoped that this will be a leading theme of environmental history in the twenty-first century.

6
Issues and Directions in Environmental History

Introduction

Issues of environmentalism, professionalism, postmodernism, and political-economic orientation, and key interpretive ideas such as environmental decline, environmental determinism, and the relative importance of anthropogenic and external causation, have been invoked to criticize environmental history, and have concerned and divided environmental historians. The debates on these issues seem unlikely to recede; rather, it is most likely that further issues will continue to arise. The following selection of issues is by no means exhaustive.

Professionalism

Looking at the field of environmental history over the past 30 years, I have noticed some trends that seem likely to continue. Professionalism has made great strides here as it has in most parts of the scholarly world. Environmental historians now are more strictly historians, although more likely than other historians to engage in interdisciplinary studies. This is reflected in a higher degree of acceptance for the subdiscipline within the historical profession, but it is to be hoped that acceptance will not lead to complacency. It may not be healthy for environmental history itself, which is by its nature an interdisciplinary subject, and arose from the stimulation of exchange between scholars in separate fields. Reviving the effort that gave birth to environmental history may be difficult, since the forms of human knowledge involved in that effort include some that are located on opposite sides of the famous cultural gulf between the sciences and the humanities,[1] but it is inescapable if environmental historians are to avoid being marooned on an island of specialization. It would be even more unfortunate if there were a feeling that those who are not trained primarily as historians cannot do acceptable work as environmental historians. Steven Pyne, President of the American Society for Environmental History, recently welcomed interchange with other disciplines:

> When ASEH members speak of "environmental history," they mean history done by professional historians, typically in the Academy, but perhaps on detached duty as public historians. The environment, however, attracts a great many scholars, and increasingly they are conceiving the subject in historical terms. Anthropologists, geographers, archaeologists, foresters – all are incorporating, or rediscovering, the valence between history and nature. Even ecology is becoming (if grudgingly) a historical science, rather like geology. Each group defines the topic in its own way, indifferent to the methodological sound and fury of the others. Collectively, they challenge environmental history; they complement it; and they offer opportunities for scholarly colonization.[2]

The survey of writing presented in the foregoing chapters should amply demonstrate that many of the finest environmental histories were written by non-historians, and that the debt of environmental history to historical geography, ecology, and other disciplines is already enormous.

Advocacy

In the writing of environmental history in recent years one senses that there is less environmental advocacy than there was in the 1960s and 1970s. John Opie once called it "the spectre of advocacy," in that environmental historians were likely to be suspect within the historical community for promoting an environmentalist point of view.[3] This observation may have been only partially warranted; as citizens, individual environmental historians were involved in local movements such as those to preserve the Indiana Dunes and the Grand Canyon, as well as national campaigns against pollution and in international non-governmental organizations such as the World Wildlife Fund. Jared Diamond, for example, has long served as a director of the last-named organization.[4] But environmental historians from the beginning were meticulous in not allowing their commitments to distort their careful and conscientious use of the historical method. Today, mistrust is not greatly warranted. Environmental historians guard their objectivity (perhaps sometimes they overcompensate in their desire to avoid an appearance of partiality), and are just as likely to be critical of environmentalists as of their opponents. John McNeill, discussing this phenomenon, observes that political engagement has declined among environmental historians in the US and Europe, but remains strong in India and Latin America.[5] Still it is undoubtedly true that most environmental historians today are aware in a positive sense that their field has roots in common with the environmental movement, and as citizens share many of its goals. Opie also reminded his audience that advocacy has certain virtues, and that to avoid it completely may be to dodge important ethical questions. To be accurate should not mean to be less committed. This fact is well illustrated by some of the most-admired environmental historians, who when their understanding of history, in the light of ethics, leads them to advise certain courses of action and warn against others, do not hesitate to say so. William Cronon has argued that environmental historians correctly do their work in the expectation of informing the makers of policy, in "The Uses of Environmental History."[6] One of the finest examples of advocacy in the literature of environmental history is Donald Worster's *The Wealth of Nature: Environmental History and the Ecological Imagination*,[7] a series of beautifully written essays, almost every one of which is a call for understanding and action based on a careful examination of history and informed by a passion for human values and a deep appreciation of the world of nature and its life. To sample the flavor of this kind of advocacy, it will be well worth the time and space to read a paragraph from that book:

> This blooming, buzzing, howling world of nature that surrounds us has always been a force in human life. It is so today, despite all our efforts to free ourselves from that dependency, and despite our frequent unwillingness to acknowledge our dependency until it is too late and a crisis is upon us. Environmental history aims to bring back into our awareness that significance of nature and, with the aid of modern science, to discover some fresh truths about ourselves and our past. We need that understanding in a great many places: for instance, in little Haiti, which has been undergoing a long, tragic spiral into poverty, disease, and land degradation, and in the rain forests of Borneo as they have passed from traditional tribal to modern corporate ownership and management. In both of those cases, the fortunes of people and land have been as inseparably connected as they have been on the Great Plains, and in both the world market economy has created or intensified an ecological problem. Whatever terrain the environmental historian chooses to investigate, he [sic] has to address the age-old predicament of how humankind can feed itself without degrading the primal source of life. Today as ever, that problem is the fundamental challenge in human ecology, and meeting it will require knowing the earth well – knowing its history and knowing its limits.[8]

Environmental Determinism

A charge often made against environmental historians is that of environmental determinism, which is the theory that history is inevitably guided by forces that are not of human origin or subject to human choice. Studies that emphasize the roles of climate and epidemic disease have been subjected in particular to this criticism. The basic conception of environmental history, however, is that of the interaction of human societies and the natural environment. The judgment as to which is more dominant or effective in the interrelationship of humans and nature has varied greatly among environmental historians. There is in fact a continuum of opinion on the subject among environmental historians from one extreme to the other. Near the environmental determinist end of the spectrum, for example, is Jared Diamond, whose background is in medicine and anthropology, and who teaches geography, but who nonetheless admits to being an environmental historian. He clearly argues the extent to which human societies are embedded in the natural matrix. In emphasizing the role of environment, he rejects the idea that some human groups are physically or intellectually superior to others. Human groups developed as they did by dealing creatively with the factors presented to them by their particular environments. At the other end of the spectrum is William Cronon, who with other authors in the volume of collected essays that he edited, *Uncommon Ground: Toward Reinventing Nature,*[9] argued that untrammeled nature no longer exists because humans have completely reshaped the planet. Wilderness, he announced, is entirely a cultural invention.[10] This is not just to say (to mix a metaphor) that the hand of man has set foot everywhere, whether through exploration or pollution or management, but that the very idea of nature is a human creation and that there is no way of relating to nature without culture. If Diamond represents environmental determinism, then perhaps Cronon represents cultural determinism. Each, however, insists that he is analyzing an interaction between nature and culture. Diamond argues for human choice and Cronon argues that nature really exists and that there is a highly meaningful human cultural interaction with it. Most environmental historians find themselves in a broad middle ground, although it is always more difficult for a scholar to define a balance than to stake out a radical position.

Presentism

Another criticism of environmental history sometimes raised by other historians is that of presentism. These critics note that awareness of environmental problems is entirely a contemporary phenomenon. The very word "environmentalism" did not emerge in general use until the 1960s, and environmental history became a recognizable subdiscipline only in the 1970s. The motive that led to the inquiry was a reaction to uniquely modern problems. Is environmental history, therefore, an untenable attempt to read late twentieth-century developments and concerns back into past historical periods in which they were not operative, and certainly not conscious to human participants during those times? The problem with this criticism is that it is fundamentally an argument against history itself as an intellectual endeavor that can be applied to the understanding of the present. Modern problems exist in their present forms because they are the results of historical processes. The relationship with nature was the earliest challenge facing humankind. It would take a particularly egregious form of denial not to see a precedent for the market economy in the exchange of a tribal nomad's meat and skins for a village agriculturalist's grain and textiles. The Greek philosopher Plato described soil erosion, and the Roman poet Horace complained about urban air pollution.[11] The Columbian transfer of Europeans along with their crops, weeds, animals, and diseases to the New World in large part explains the history and present state of the Americas.[12] The study of past effects of environmental forces on human societies, and the impact of human activities on the environment, gives needed perspective to the dilemmas of the contemporary world.[13]

Declensionist Narratives

Yet another criticism, and one often heard at historical conferences, is that works written by environmental historians tend to be 'declensionist' narratives, that is, they describe a process by which a reasonably beneficial environmental situation became progressively worse due to human actions. For example, the Valley of Mezquital in Mexico, a highly productive agricultural region when farmed by the pre-Columbian Otomí people, was transformed through overgrazing by

Spanish sheep into "an almost mythologically poor place renowned for its aridity, for the poverty of its indigenous inhabitants, and for exploitation by large landowners," according to a compelling account written by Elinor Melville.[14] The biologically rich tropical forests of Brazil's Atlantic coastal region were hacked away from the time of discovery by Europeans down to the present, as another exemplary environmental history by Warren Dean, *With Broadax and Firebrand*, puts it.[15] Today these forests are represented by scattered fragments, ostensibly protected by Brazilian law but still under attack in various forms. When expanded to the world scale, such regional examples become a story of global degradation, and it is hard to avoid a prediction of worldwide catastrophe, still more so where phenomena such as global warming are concerned. Since the process of destruction is still going on, and increasing exponentially in scale, it seems logical to extrapolate the trend toward future disaster. The declensionist narrative may even appear to have cautionary value. In the Middle Ages the Church taught an eschatology including the abolition of the earthly order and the Last Judgment of souls, and this was thought to frighten believers into good behavior. Is environmental catastrophism simply the secular replacement for religious eschatology in world history? Of course historians generally avoid the future like the plague, since earlier historians who ventured to describe coming events often turned out to be spectacularly wrong – look at H. G. Wells, who predicted world order and lasting peace after World War I[16] – and environmental historians are no exception. Generally they resolve only to describe what has happened already and leave speculation to the reader, even when they secretly expect the worst to happen. Sometimes they break this resolution, however.[17] If history is generally held by its practitioners to exclude many forms of prediction, the validity of science is held to be tested by the accuracy of its predictions, and environmental history is, among historical subfields, perhaps uniquely open to the insights of science. To complicate the matter, however, the science most relevant to environmental history is ecology, and ecology is a historical science in which predictions are notoriously difficult to make, if not also undependable. Environmental historians are sharply aware of this conundrum, however, and the charge of unsupportable catastrophism is on the whole unwarranted. The criticism of declensionist narration may be met in large part by the observation that deterioration of the global environment as a result of human activities is a fact revealed by careful research in many cases. To describe them otherwise would be to ignore the evidence.

Political-Economic Theory

Environmental historians, along with historians in general, have sometimes been accused of being light on theory. The charge probably has validity across the field, although there have been some notable exceptions, among them Carolyn Merchant in "The Theoretical Structure of Ecological Revolutions,"[18] and Madhav Gadgil and Ramachandra Guha in "A Theory of Ecological History," the first section of their book, *This Fissured Land*.[19] One of the most trenchant and stimulating critics of environmental history is the sociologist and economist James O'Connor, who published "What is Environmental History? Why Environmental History?" along with other relevant essays in a collection, *Natural Causes*,[20] in 1998. He takes environmental historians to task for not recognizing how revolutionary their kind of history is. O'Connor maintains that:

> environmental history may be regarded as the culmination of all previously existing histories – assuming we include environmental dimensions of contemporary political, economic, and cultural history, as well as environmental history strictly defined. Far from the marginal subject so many historians still regard it to be, environmental history is (or should be) at the very center of historiography today.

His implicit criticism is that environmental historians have either not realized, or if they have realized it, not explained how theoretically central and revolutionary their endeavor is. It places history within the context that actually envelops it: the physical reality of the natural world and the material bases and limitations of civilization. "Sustainability" has been embraced as a desideratum, but a satisfactory ecological definition of the term is elusive. O'Connor asks if sustainable capitalism is possible, and answers that it is not, because capitalism entails profit and accumulation, which are possible only under conditions of growth that will destroy ecosystems and exhaust natural resources. This is, in simplified terms, what O'Connor calls "The Second Contradiction of Capitalism."[21] Critics of O'Connor would point out that he is a Marxist and therefore would be expected to attack capitalism. But his criticism extends as well to Marx, who wrote in a pre-ecological age and did not appreciate the fundamental role of the productive forces of nature's economy. The result is that, as O'Connor put it, "Historical materialism is also not materialistic enough."[22] In the face of this double contradiction, he advises environmental historians to recognize that their craft:

> is turning out to be political, economic, and social history – widened, deepened, and made more inclusive . . . One can be sure that environmental history will be reinterpreted, even revolutionized, by future generations of historians, in light of new problems, techniques, sources, and so on, but also of revolutions in political, economic, and social history themselves, to which environmental history is contributing today.[23]

The Next Issues

A number of issues have been identified as worthy of more attention by environmental historians, areas where there is both need and opportunity for future work. For example, a forum on the subject, "What's Next for Environmental History?"[24] in the January 2005 number of *Environmental History* includes brief essays by 29 leading environmental historians, not all from the US, on directions they detect in and/or recommend for writing in the field in the present and immediate future. John McNeill, in an article not in that collection, calls issues like these "paths not (much) taken,"[25] and for him they include military dimensions, soils history, mining, migrations, and the environmental history of the sea. I will comment on a number of these, beginning with four themes selected from those I regard as most important for the environment and environmentalism in the coming decades. These are growth of population, the declining power of local communities over their own environments, the history of energy and energy resources, and loss of biodiversity. Following these, I will select a few of the many topics suggested in various articles by colleagues.

Population growth

While population is an unavoidable element in many of their narratives, environmental historians are hesitant to address it directly. The reasons are not hard to find: assigning a major role to population growth as a cause of environmental degradation can open an author to the charge of racism or Malthusianism, the idea that population growth will inevitably exceed the food production necessary to sustain it. But the historical trend is clear. Ten thousand years ago, there were only five to ten million humans on Earth. The United Nations observed the day of birth of the six billionth living human on October 12, 1999, and conservatively predicted that we shall reach 8.9 billion by 2050, with more than 90 percent of that increase in the developing nations. Population growth is the most potent engine driving environmental destruction. Burgeoning population adds to the scale of environmental effects caused by humans, and makes changes happen faster. One village near a forest might use so little firewood that it could continue to do so forever, but ten villages would exceed sustainable yield and destroy the forest in ten years. This is not theoretical; it is happening in much of the tropical world.

People in poorer countries do less damage per capita, but even a small amount of resource use becomes major when multiplied by millions or billions, and they can afford fewer restorative measures. In the industrial countries, the environmental footprint of each inhabitant is bigger, so that even a small population increase causes correspondingly greater impact. Recent declines in the rate of population increase are

16. Schoolchildren and teachers visiting the Red Fort, Delhi, India. One of the most important results of population growth is the need for education, including environmental education.
Photograph taken by the author in 1992.

believed to result from improving health and education, availability of birth control, higher standards of living, and the increasing participation of women in reproductive decisions. But population expansion in developing countries undercuts some of these positive factors. If this occurs, the UN predictions will prove conservative indeed. There are precedents in environmental history. When such an upward swing of population pushing the limits of resources has occurred, as happened in the southern Maya lowlands between 650 and 850 CE, and in Europe during the two centuries before 1300, it was followed by a crash and the abandonment of many settlements. Without measures to curb population growth, along with controls on pollution and resource use, a demographic crash later in the twenty-first century or shortly beyond seems likely. The history of surges and crashes in population demands attention from environmental historians. An excellent treatment of "Neo-Malthusianism" is by Björn-Ola Linnér, *The Return of*

Malthus.[26] Otis Graham has written a textbook on the post-World War II US that emphasizes population, resources, and the environment.[27]

Local versus global determination of policy

The course of the relationship between culture and nature is determined to a major extent by the scale on which decisions about environmental policy are made. Does a local community make its own choices about what will happen to its environment? Or are the operative decisions made on national, regional, or even global levels? The direction of the trend through history seems clear, and the need for environmental historians to investigate its course seems clear. Local determination, already weakened in respect to national and colonial power, passed into the shadow of global power in the twentieth century, when a number of international institutions transformed the world market economy. The financial experts of capitalist nations erected a structure to encourage free trade and open resources of the world, renewable and nonrenewable, to exploitation. These include the International Monetary Fund and the World Bank, and the General Agreement on Tariffs and Trade (GATT). GATT's supervising body, the World Trade Organization (WTO) with a membership of over 150 nations including the largest ones, can make a claim to oversight of the world economy. WTO is committed to ceaseless growth and has not stressed environmental protection. Indeed, WTO decisions have nullified national bans on products considered environmentally damaging.

As global institutions and multinational corporations become more powerful, nations, especially in the third world, become smaller as colonial empires split apart and separatist movements succeed. They face powerful supranational organizations that can summon up huge amounts of money and numbers of employees greater than those of the governments concerned, and can promise jobs and other rewards. Local people are seldom skilled in the jobs demanded by the corporations, however, who bring in workers from outside who do not share local attitudes and customs. Virtually all these factors operated in the case of the island of Nauru, where exploitation of phosphates for fertilizer resulted in the destruction of forests and other biota, transforming most of the island into uninhabitable wasteland, as an environmental history by Carl McDaniel and John Gowdy, *Paradise for Sale*, chronicles.[28] Elsewhere, government programs to encourage exports, rising prices of timber and other wood products, and depletion of accessible forests, drove multi-national logging concerns to seek out new resources. The effect on local peoples who depend on forests has been catastrophic.

But the biggest demand for resources and the greatest influx of population are seen in urban areas. Cities in less industrialized countries grow most rapidly, and slums make up most of this growth. In Cairo, to give one instance, people actually live in cemeteries and garbage dumps. The vision of a third-world megalopolis with a rapidly growing population straining an inadequate infrastructure threatens to make the concept of a local community meaningless. Most of the

17. Wood chipping of Australian trees for export to Japan, in George Town, Tasmania, Australia. Free trade and the world market economy produce environmental impacts at great distance from points of demand.
Photograph taken by the author in 1996.

future technological advances that can be envisioned seem likely to strengthen anti-local powers. In the face of this trend, environmental historians can look for case studies of local models of city planning such as Curitiba, Brazil, where planning parks, pedestrian malls, public transport, garbage and recycling systems make it an ecological success and a great place to live, and where grassroots movements have succeeded.

Turning to the global side, perhaps environmental historians will see UN programs worthy of further study. Several agencies have work on environmental health. Others have limited maritime pollution and the killing of whales. UNESCO's Man and the Biosphere Program has established biosphere reserves planned to encourage local peoples to engage in traditional economic activities in buffer zones. The UN Environment Program (UNEP) fostered the erection of a framework of international environmental law through such agreements as the 1987 Montreal Protocol on Substances That Deplete the Ozone Layer, one of the most successful international environmental treaties.

Energy and resources

The history of energy and energy resources is another area where there is room for new studies in environmental history. The use of energy by human societies has increased substantially since the onset of the Industrial Revolution, but in the twentieth century an unprecedented exponential growth began and still continues. The environmental history of energy use has been the story of the exploitation of a series of resources as technology granted access to them, one after another. The first industrial fuel was wood, including charcoal, a use that placed great demands on the forest resource. European governments, perceiving an incipient timber crisis due to fuel demands in the early modern period, enacted a series of laws intended to ensure the supply of timber for essential purposes such as naval construction. An example is the French Forest Ordinance of 1669, which turned forestry into a branch of the state-managed economy and restricted production of charcoal, as Michael Williams notes.[29]

The shift from wood, which is at least theoretically a renewable resource, to non-renewable fossil fuels occurred during the second half of the nineteenth century. Perhaps that development provided a reprieve for European forests, although pollution worsened. Coal became the dominant fuel for industry and transportation first in Europe and North America and then through much of the world, but with the internal combustion engine in the twentieth century, coal's primacy was challenged by petroleum and natural gas, which matched or exceeded the energy production of coal by mid-century. This epoch continues today, but there are indications that it will not survive the twenty-first century, and that is a salient reason for its importance as a theme in environmental history as we consider the future.

Biodiversity

A third theme that has not escaped the attention of environmental historians, but will compel further study in the coming decades, is the preservation or destruction of the great orchestra of species that makes up the biodiversity of life on Earth. Interaction with countless kinds of animals and plants helped to form our bodies and minds, and shaped historical developments such as hunting and agriculture. Human actions have reduced the number of species, and the number of individual organisms within most species, diminishing biodiversity and the complexity of ecosystems. This happened from early times through Roman roundups of animals for their amphitheaters and the commercial "world hunt" of modern Europeans described by John F. Richards in *The Unending Frontier*[30] to the destruction of habitats, depletion of fisheries and whale populations, and the saddening killing of great apes for bush meat in Africa and Indonesia at present. By the end of the twentieth century, extinctions were occurring on a scale only matched by catastrophes of the geological record. In recent years, scientists, writers, and others have recognized a crisis of biodiversity. Concern often appeared over the danger to single species: the spotted owl in the US northwest, the panda in China, the tiger in India and Siberia, and the elephant in Africa. These are highly visible indicator

18. Giant pandas in the Panda Research Station, Wolong, Sichuan Province, China. Attempts to preserve and regenerate endangered species such as this are a twentieth-century development of the conservation movement.
Photograph taken by the author in 1988.

species, but the real problem in each case is the diminution of the ecosystem to which each of them belongs. It is a process called "habitat destruction," but is really the fragmentation of communities of life, since those communities lose their complexity as they shrink in area and relinquish many of the species that were members of them. The subsidy the economy has been taking from wild nature may be near an end.[31] as the last wild places yield to the advance of tree farms, industrial agriculture, strip mines, power plants, and urban sprawl. The effect on human history needs to be understood.

Evolution and biotechnology

The historian Edmund Russell authored an article, "Evolutionary History: Prospectus for a New Field," in 2003,[32] in which he argues that environmental historians, except for

Jared Diamond and a few others like him, have been too narrow in their use of biology. They have paid attention to ecology, he says, but have pretty much ignored evolution. This is not because they have trouble with the idea of evolution by natural selection; like all scientifically informed scholars in the twenty-first century, they accept Darwin's basic idea as the most reasonable way of explaining how species change and originate. But, like Darwin, many of them have probably thought of evolution as a slow process involving minute changes over long periods of geologic time (outside historical time), and therefore unlikely to affect history on the timescale of human events within a lifetime or a few generations. Such an attitude is now outmoded. Even evolution through natural selection works more rapidly than Darwin appreciated, as studies of the finches by the biologists Peter and Rosemary Grant on the island of Daphne Major in the Galápagos Archipelago have shown.[33] Of course, Darwin was a careful student of the artificial selection that produced breeds of domestic animals such as pigeons and dogs in relatively short time scales. It is now evident that humans are inadvertently accelerating evolution by doing things like applying pesticides and using antibiotics. By killing the sensitive organisms and sparing the resistant ones, humans have cause the survival of strains that are the fittest in resisting the very weapons that we use against them in defense of our crops and our own bodies. The results in the economic and health spheres are major. DDT was effective in the years after World War II, but the insects evolved resistance, and now we perforce use other chemicals that are temporarily effective. There are staphylococci that (metaphorically) laugh at penicillin.

So much for the Darwinian aspect of evolution. Today, however, the Mendelian aspect presents the operation of a historical force that is potentially as great or even greater. Now that humans understand the genetic basis of heredity, and are able to manipulate genes to produce "designer crops," we can circumvent the cumbersome process of selection. Genetic engineers are making varieties of living species that selection of either kind did not produce, and possibly never could have produced. Biotechnology can and will have effects both on culture and nature, and environmental historians

19. "Lonesome George," the sole remaining giant tortoise of the Pinta Island species, in the Charles Darwin Research Center on Santa Cruz Island, Galápagos Islands, Ecuador. The birds in the foreground are examples of the famous "Darwin's finches."
Photograph taken by the author in 1996.

will have to explain those effects, or other scholars will have to do it for them.[34]

Oceans and seas

The South African historian Lance van Sittert calls for environmental historians to concern themselves with what he calls "The Other Seven-Tenths" of the globe.[35] The world ocean constitutes most of the Earth's surface, and an even greater proportion of the biosphere. The Pacific Ocean alone covers one-third of the globe. Human use of the great bodies of saltwater includes transportation, trade, fisheries and other consumption of marine life including the great whales, and extraction of resources. Some human communities actually live on the seas. Looking back through history, the seas were the place of origin of life, avenues for the peopling of the islands, and the open ways for discovery, colonization, and slavery. They have tested and killed seafarers, and are the spawning grounds for storms by whatever names they are called: cyclones, typhoons, hurricanes. Nations have claimed territories in the seas, and international negotiation has created laws of the sea. Dangers of pollution, overfishing, extinctions and the destruction of coral reefs have raised concern around the world.

With such a vast opportunity for study, it is disappointing that environmental historians have not written more about it. In fact, they often treat "land" and "landscape" as synonyms for the whole environment. Works like Braudel's *Mediterranean*[36] are really histories of the lands around a sea rather than the sea itself. Admirable exceptions include Arthur McEvoy in works like *The Fisherman's Problem*.[37] A conference, "Environmental History and the Oceans," was held in Copenhagen in 2004. But an environmental history of the ocean remains to be written.

20. Mangroves in the estuary of the Aganashini River near Kumta, Uttara Kannada, Karnataka State, India. Mangroves provide important shelter for fish spawning, but are being removed in many parts of the world for shrimp farming and other developments.
     Photograph taken by the author in 1997.

Conclusion

The global environmental problems that first aroused the attention and interest of historians in environmental history have increased both in intensity and in number, and the interpretive value of environmental history has received wide acceptance. Nature and culture are, after all, interpenetrating notions that cannot be understood apart from one another. It is also notable that the number of scholars, particularly young scholars, engaged in the research and writing of environmental history has grown exponentially over the decades since 1980, and the list of nations where communities of such scholars exist has also grown. Environmental history seems certain to continue to influence the writing of history in the remaining years of the twenty-first century. As Ellen Stroud puts it piquantly in a recent article which claims that environmental history is not merely a subfield of history, but an interpretive tool that stands ready for use by all historians, "If other historians would join us in our attention to the physical, biological, and ecological nature of dirt, water, air, trees, and animals (including humans), they would find themselves led to new questions and new answers about the past."[38]

7
Thoughts on Doing Environmental History

Introduction

This chapter consists of suggestions for study of, research on, and writing about environmental history. It is intended for those who are interested in the subject, but are as yet relatively unfamiliar with it. That group would include undergraduate students, graduate students who are comparatively new to environmental history, and perhaps even scholars in other fields who would like to add environmental history to their tool kits. It is by no means a complete guide to environmental history – that would require a book substantially more generously proportioned than this volume – but a number of hints that students and other writers may find helpful.

Guidance in Methodology

I will start by recommending a handful of works on how to do environmental history by masters of the craft that can provide useful guidance. Widely mentioned, and deservedly so, is Donald Worster's appendix to his collection, *The Ends of the Earth*, "Doing Environmental History."[1] More recent, and more detailed, is Carolyn Merchant's *Columbia Guide* to *American Environmental History.*[2] Although it is limited to US environmental history, much of Merchant's advice is applicable either directly or by analogy to those working on other parts of the world. One of her greatest contributions is in pointing out the kinds of questions that environmental historians ask, or could ask. Merchant has also created a CD that serves as a practical technological supplement to the volume, although it is a separate product.[3] William Cronon's article, "A Place for Stories: Nature, History, and Narrative," contains some principles that can clarify the task of writing an environmental history narrative.[4] For those desiring an approach from historical geography, and a non-American one at that, I. G. Simmons' *Environmental History: A Concise Introduction*[5] certainly can be recommended.

Worster's article calls for environmental historians to escape the limitations of most traditional history, and to deepen "our understanding of how humans have been affected by their natural environment through time and, conversely, how they have affected that environment and with what results."[6] In doing so, environmental history will pursue three lines of inquiry, not separately but as components of an integrated study. The first Worster identifies as an attempt to understand nature itself in the changes it exhibits; that is, on one level, environmental history takes cognizance of the history of the environment *per se.* The second inquiry involves human economic activities and social organization and the effects they have on the environment, including the power that various parts of the social hierarchy have to make decisions about these activities. Finally, the third level of study includes all the thoughts, feelings, and intuitions that humans and their societies have about nature, including science, philosophy, law, and religion. Each of these levels of inquiry requires that environmental historians outfit themselves with tools formerly considered to belong to disciplines other than history. The first implies the need for understanding the natural sciences, most importantly ecology. For the second level, the tools come from the study of technology, anthropology and its subfield cultural ecology, and economics. The third level, of perceptions and values, involves the humanities and a wide range of ideas, although "the actual effects of such ideas, in the past or in the present, are extremely difficult to trace empirically,"[7] and ideas about nature in any given society are usually complex and to one extent or another contradictory. Finally, Worster emphasizes the importance of the relationship between history and geography: historians concentrate on time and geographers on space, but neither must "lose sight of the elemental human–nature connection."[8] Worster has given us a tall order, having appropriated as tools for environmental history if not all, at least a very large proportion of all the methods used in every corner of academia. We study humans and nature; therefore can anything human or natural be outside our inquiry? The challenge is daunting, but we must not lose courage in face of it.

Carolyn Merchant may offer ways of proceeding in face of the challenge, pointing out five approaches to doing environmental history that summarize the methods of most of its practitioners without exhausting the possibilities. The first concentrates on human interactions with the biological aspects of the environment, including ecosystems. The second analyzes the differences between levels of "human interactions with nature, such as ecology, production, reproduction, and ideas."[9] The third approach emphasizes environmental politics and economics, and land and resource use policy. The fourth, like Worster's third level, looks at the history of ideas about nature, and the fifth, similar to Cronon's outline discussed below, proceeds on the basis of the notion that environmental histories are narratives, that is, stories that are told about humans and nature, stories that may have cautionary points about past human experiences with nature and advice about present and future decisions.

Cronon's counsel on doing environmental history is rich, varied, and controversial, and impossible to summarize here. I will limit my comments to the principles enunciated in the article mentioned above, "A Place for Stories: Nature, History, and Narrative," which are especially clear and useful. Cronon maintains that environmental historians, like all historians, frame their accounts of history as stories. In telling stories, historians select the elements that make up the story line, and thus cross the boundary between the natural and the artificial. But even so, historians are not free to make up any stories they like; not all stories are equally valid representations of the past. There are constraints on storytelling, and Cronon urges three.

First, "stories cannot contravene known facts about the past."[10] He gives an example: a story of Great Plains history as continuous progress without mentioning the Dust Bowl would be bad history.

Second, environmental historians have a particular constraint, since they believe that nature really exists beyond their narratives, and that is that their "stories must make ecological sense."[11] They cannot ignore or falsify the records and workings of the ecosystems in their living and non-living aspects. This implies that the environmental historian must know the ecology of the time and place about which the story is told.

Finally, to paraphrase very slightly, the third constraint is that historians write as members of communities, and therefore must take those communities into account as they do their work.[12] On one level, this means that scholars must take one another and their valid criticisms into account in the process of constructing a narrative. On another level, at least to me, it means that environmental historians have a responsibility to the wider audience of the human community, since their work helps to provide the awareness necessary for deliberations concerning the decisions that society must make in terms of the environmental crises it faces.

I. G. Simmons envisions environmental history as a method combining scientific and humanistic approaches and mediating the two. There is a cultural ecology and a natural ecology, and each has its stages or successions. Environmental history investigates the course of their interactions in time, and their effects on one another, although it will understandably find the effects of culture on nature more problematic and interesting than the reverse. Cultural ecology historically goes through a number of stages characterized by different interactions with the environment, although the changes are not uniform throughout the world, since some regions lag behind others. These are hunting–gathering and early agriculture, riverine civilizations, agricultural empires, the Atlantic-industrial era, and the Pacific-global era. Natural ecology also goes through a number of stages in succession, granted that they differ in various parts of the world and that ecologists increasingly recognize complexity and randomness in the process of succession. In history, these ecologies interact with one another, and the result is a global mosaic of places where the natural and the cultural predominate to various degrees. The idea of "climax," in which a stable and self-renewing ecological community replaces the intervening stages, is now problematic. There are few such places remaining on Earth. "The ways in which human societies alter the natural world are wonderfully various," says Simmons,[13] and describes categories of human actions on ecosystems. These include deflection (keeping natural succession at an early stage that is found valuable to a human group), simplification, obliteration, domestication, diversification (including introduction of exotic species), and conservation. He provides examples of these processes in ecosystems from various parts of the world, and discusses the meaning of "wilderness" as nature less affected by human change, and attitudes to it. His last paragraph is worth quoting:

> we are creatures of evolution on cosmic, ecological and cultural scales. We are also creators on the last two of these. But in none is there a break-point which would enable us to ignore what had gone before. History is like a narrative tapestry: if we cut it up and store some of it in a chest, we shall not understand the message of what is left for us to see hanging on the wall.[14]

Environmental history refuses to cut culture from nature. Equally it must not cut history from geography.

The Search for Sources

Those who describe the historical method (used by all historians) always emphasize the importance of the search for sources of evidence. Among sources, as a rule, the closer to the time, place, and people being studied, the better. By and large, they are talking about written sources, in some cases supplemented by oral interviews when that is possible. What could be better than a primary source: for example, an original diary in which a general recorded his thoughts on the eve of a battle? Better, possibly, than a secondary account written later on by someone who had not seen the engagement. Of course an environmental historian will rightly be expected to understand and use the historical method, and to gather all the written sources that can possibly illuminate the question under investigation. For environmental historians, these sources will include not only all the relevant books and articles, but as the case dictates, business records, scientific reports, newspaper records, and literature revealing the attitudes of people of the times. Websites can be enormously helpful, but are inherently more ephemeral than material published in hard copy; that is, the site may not be there when the researcher tries to access it again, or the desired pages may have been erased.

However, an environmental historian also has another obligation, and that is to become familiar with the place. The land knows the truth, as a Pacific Islander aphorism has it. The territory has a tale to tell. The landscape is a book whose pages, even when they are palimpsests, can be read. It is, naturally, necessary to know the language, and that means acquiring tools that may only be obtainable outside history departments. It may be possible to write a good environmental history of a country one has not even visited, but that would entail many difficulties and potential errors. It is a task I would seriously try to avoid. If it is at all possible, see the place. The writer can learn much by exposing the senses to the unique qualities of a region: the scent of the sea wind on a mountaintop in Oregon, the water-drip trill of oropendulas returning to their nest in the rainforest of the Peruvian Amazon, the peculiar mosaic patterns of Tuscany's vineyards and fields, the sandy ground underfoot shaking from the pounding of giant waves out there on Mo'orea's offshore coral reef, the taste of the sweet water inside a coconut on a hot day in a spice garden in Karnataka. Perhaps not one of these would make it to the pages of a book or essay, but each of them inform when combined with all the other minutiae of that particular place that do not ordinarily come from reading.

It is true that one cannot visit the past, except in memory. I have a friend and colleague who has spent an entire academic career studying and teaching about ancient Greece, but has never visited Greece on any of numerous trips to Europe. When I asked why, I got the answer, "Pericles is no longer at home." True, and the present landscape around Athens is not the one the Athenians gazed upon in the Golden Age of the fifth century BC. There are fewer trees, and a metropolis perhaps six times the size of the ancient one fills the bowl between the mountains. But an environmental historian can get a sense of how things must have been, and trace classical lineaments in the modern scene. The heights of Mount Pentelicus and Mount Hymettos, the sources respectively of marble and honey, still reflect the evening sunlight, and the sea, surely one of the greatest environmental influences on the life of Athens, still surrounds the peninsula of Attica on three sides. One can still make a meal of olives, bread, and wine, the staple crops of the Mediterranean in ancient and modern times.

The environment itself can offer valuable evidence beyond that found in written sources. The increasing technological sophistication of archaeology has enabled the mapping of farms, fields, and industrial enterprises such as sugar plantations. Microscopic examination can now identify the species of fragments of wood or charcoal, and dendrochronology can show the dates of rafters used in buildings. Palynology, the examination of deposits of pollen in deposits on lake bottoms and in caves and other relatively undisturbed places, can trace the history of vegetation in the local environment, giving evidence of forest loss and recovery and the changing patterns of agricultural crops over the years. Studies of sedimentation can provide estimates of rates of erosion and the sources of eroded materials. Ice cores from the Antarctic and Greenland have yielded information on climate as well as atmospheric gases and pollutants from air trapped in the layers of snowfall deposited over past time periods. Environmental historians can find corroborating and/or challenging information in scientific reports of these investigations, although it may take learning a new vocabulary and the principles of statistics to do so.

In fact, an environmental historian may well develop an enthusiasm for the manifold interests once embraced under the title of natural history, a desire to observe, identify, and understand the geology, climate, plants, and animal species of the area studied. Here field books and direct observations, as well as museum collections and records, may prove valuable. As a geological example, someone investigating the urban environmental history of New Orleans needs to know that the underlying stratum includes alluvial soil that shrinks on drying, a fact which explains why much of the city lies below sea level, creating a chronic drainage problem and setting the stage for disastrous flooding. This unstable aspect of the city's environment was noted well before the 2005 Hurricane Katrina by the environmental historian Ari Kelman in *A River and Its City*,[15] and by the historical geographer Craig Colten in *An Unnatural Metropolis*.[16] Both authors show that hurricanes with attendant death, disease, and displacement were recurring aspects of the city's environmental existence long before 2005. Kelman in particular sees a two-sided relationship between city and river in which the city depends on the river for commerce but tries to insulate itself, turning its back on the river that flows beside and above it. Familiarity with the living species in an area is a prerequisite to any discussion of the detailed historical operation of the ecology there. Which species are wild and long endemic to the local landscape, and which are introductions by human agency, either as domesticates, some of which may have escaped and survived in a feral state, or as exotic species that have been released into the natural environment? In Hawai'i, for instance, the *koa* tree with its prized wood evolved locally, the taro (*kalo*) plant was brought in by the Polynesian settlers in their double-hulled canoes, and the invasive fire-adapted fountain grass, native to Africa, was first planted as an ornamental garden plant in Hawai'i in the early twentieth century and subsequently spread over vast tracts of ranchlands and lava fields. Some sense of the environment as it existed at a past time chosen as a baseline will enable the changes caused since by human activities to be estimated.

Resources

Increasingly, libraries have made efforts to establish or enlarge their collections in environmental history. As one would expect, these tend to be those at universities that are home to a program in environmental history and/or a recognized scholar in the subject. Among these are California, Duke, Kansas, Wisconsin, and Maine in the US, not to mention the Library of Congress; the British Library and the universities of Oxford, Cambridge, Durham, St Andrews and Stirling in the UK; the Australian National University; the University of Otago in New Zealand; and the University of South Africa. For US environmental history, the Conservation Library of the Denver Public Library in Denver, Colorado, has actively resumed its long-standing program of acquisition, and sponsors fellowships for researchers in the field. Most worthy of note is the library of the Forest History Society in Durham, North Carolina, associated with Duke University. It has probably the world's largest and most accessible collection on Forest History, and also has made a major expansion into environmental history generally. Its holdings include a unique store of photographs and oral histories. It also has assembled a splendid bibliography of forest, conservation, and environmental history. Its holdings are searchable in a user-friendly website.[17] The European Society for Environmental History is assembling a bibliography, also web-searchable.[18] Of course, the needs for research for any given environmental history topic are unique and when searching for a library in which to work, it is obviously important to make careful inquiry about the strengths and weaknesses of a collection in light of those needs. The foregoing chapters have suggestions on bibliographical resources in many of the geographical and subject fields of environmental history. The bibliographies in recommended books on environmental history, particularly recent ones, will probably also be of help. Where there are only notes instead of a bibliography, somewhat more searching may be required, but with the advantage that notes are usually keyed to discussion in the text.

Nothing prepares a writer in environmental history better than carefully reading books that can serve as models of work in the field. They can be classics that have stood the test of time and provoked thoughtful reviews, or new works, perhaps controversial ones that are on the cutting edge of scholarship and methodology. This can be true even if the works deal with a subject other than the one the researcher is pursuing. I hope that this book will help to identify some authors in environmental history that can serve as such models, but as is always the case in academia, any choice can be argued, and I am sure I have left unmentioned a number of admirable and indeed superior names through no intent of my own. Certain names, of course, almost universally occur in lists of the recognized leaders in environmental history, and these understandably tend to be those whose reputations were established in the last quarter of the twentieth century. You can find some of them in the bibliography near the end of this volume. But brilliant, readable new works are published every month in the present energetic state of the field by younger or previously unrecognized scholars who have approaches, methods, insights, and writing styles that also could well be emulated. Find them, too, and read them. Be inspired.

The people who write these books are not just authors. They are, by and large, interesting people who are, as time and opportunity permit, open and willing to share their insights. One way to appreciate the culture of environmental history is to attend the conferences and meetings where environmental historians present their findings and question and criticize one another. Of course, at least half of what goes on at an academic conference happens outside the formal sessions where papers are read, in the halls, nearby restaurants and bars, *ad hoc* meetings announced by notes on bulletin boards and word of mouth, and on field trips to places of environmental and historical interest. For example, in planned excursions during the ESEH meetings, I have visited a Scottish fishing village, a Czech castle, and a Florentine map archive, all with congenial groups. A group of associations, almost all of which hold periodic conferences, usually either annual or biennial, have as of this writing formed the International Consortium of Environmental History Organizations (ICE-HO), and there are plans in the works for a mega-meeting co-sponsored by all of them. The organizations now belonging, and there is every reason to think that the number will grow, are the American Society for Environmental History, the Australian Environmental History Network, the Australian Forest History Society, the

European Society for Environmental History, the Forest History Society, the Forest History Research Group of the International Union of Forest Research Organizations, the International Water History Association, and the Otago University History Department (New Zealand). Information on all of these is available through links on the Forest History Society website.[19] Also, a look at, or even joining, the list of the H-Environment Discussion Network[20] will bring book reviews, news, and much information, some of it very useful.

Conclusion: The Future of Environmental History

Environmental history is a rapidly growing field. As John McNeill lamented, "no mortal can keep pace with it."[21] He should know, since he has made a valiant effort to do just that. Rapid growth is characteristic of young organisms, and is ordinarily followed by maturity and even decline, but in the case of a human activity, growth will continue as long as there are needs to be filled. It seems that there are needs for environmental history, and they are needs that are not likely to disappear in the foreseeable future.

The history profession has a constant need for new perspectives such as those provided by environmental history if it is to remain intellectually alive and interesting to students and public, who after all are its consumers and patrons. Fortunately, after an initial period of resistance, the profession has opened its meetings and journals to an approach that challenges older methods and received wisdom. Classes in environmental history and positions that include it in job descriptions have appeared in universities in several countries. The ideas and approaches of environmental history have added a dimension to writing in the established subdisciplines of history, and the question, "What is environmental history?" is now a philosophical inquiry among historians instead of the annoyed challenge it sometimes was, even if giving a definitive answer remains no less difficult.

Another good reason for the persistence of environmental history is the fact that it provides an opening for interdisciplinary thought, and for cooperation between scholars with different disciplinary backgrounds. It has certainly brought a number of geographers and historians to realize how much can be accomplished on ground they share. A good study of this phenomenon is Alan H. R. Baker's *Geography and History: Bridging the Divide.*[22] *Geographical Review*, journal of the American Geographical Society, published a special issue, "Historical Geography and Environmental History" in 1998, including an introduction with the same title by Craig E. Colten and a fine article by Michael Williams, "The End of Modern History?"[23] Also see, by Williams, "The Relations of Environmental History and Historical Geography."[24] A considerably wider chasm, that between history and the science of ecology, has called out for bridge-building. A few environmental historians have attempted it, notably Donald Worster in *Nature's Economy.*[25] There has been less movement than one would hope from the scientific side of the divide, but among a few excellent studies, Frank B. Golley's *A History of the Ecosystem Concept in Ecology*[26] is surely worth mentioning. Many other interstices remain that can be filled by environmental historians and their counterparts elsewhere.

Perhaps the most pressing reason for the continuing growth of environmental history is the assured persistence and expansion of environmental concern, deriving from the growing sense among many thoughtful commentators throughout the Earth that increasing human impact upon the living systems of the planet is bringing us no closer to utopia, but instead to a crisis of survival. Looking ahead to the remaining decades of the twenty-first century, it seems certain that several themes will continue to characterize the process of change in the world environment. Among them is population growth, a multiplier of human pressure on the Earth; its rate of increase is slowing, but it has reached a size unprecedented in history and continues to expand in absolute terms. Another is the conflict between local social entities and larger ones (national and international) in the determination of policies affecting the environment. For example, a small nation facing a multinational corporation may find itself unable to control the exploitation of its own land and forests. A third theme includes multiple threats to biodiversity, including the extinction of species of plants and animals, the introduction of aggressive exotic species, and the multifarious, poorly understood effects of genetically engineered organisms. A fourth is the narrowing gap between the supply of and demand for energy and materials, including essentials such as water, and the possible virtual exhaustion of some resources. Each of these themes presents a challenge and together, along with others, they test human creativity, asking what kinds of changes might constitute a positive response. It is unfortunate that a reason for the increasing relevance of environmental history arises from a human misfortune that may prove more difficult to ameliorate than war, terrorism, or economic injustice. In the search for an answer, environmental history can give an essential perspective, offering knowledge of the historical process that led to the present situation, examples of past problems and solutions, and an analysis of the historical forces that must be dealt with. Without that perspective, decision-making falls prey to short-term political considerations based on narrow special interests. Environmental history can be a salutary corrective to easy answers.

Notes

Chapter 1 Defining Environmental History

1 Donald Worster, "Doing Environmental History," in *The Ends of the Earth: Perspectives on Modern Environmental History*, edited by Donald Worster. Cambridge: Cambridge University Press, 1988, pp. 289–307. The quotation is on p. 290.

2 William Cronon, "A Place for Stories: Nature, History, and Narrative," *The Journal of American History* 78, 4 (March 1992): 1347–76. The quotation is on p. 1373.

3 Warren Dean, *With Broadax and Firebrand: The Destruction of the Brazilian Atlantic Forest*. Berkeley and Los Angeles, CA: University of California Press, 1995.

4 Jared Diamond, *Guns, Germs, and Steel: The Fates of Human Societies*. New York: W. W. Norton, 1997.

5 Hippocrates, *Airs, Waters, Places*, edited and translated by W. H. S. Jones. Cambridge, MA: Harvard University Press, 1923.

6 William H. McNeill, *Plagues and Peoples*. Garden City, NY: Anchor Press, 1976.

7 Alfred W. Crosby, Jr., *The Columbian Exchange: Biological and Cultural Consequences of 1492*. Westport, CT: Greenwood Press, 1972. Republication with new material, Westport, CT: Praeger Publishers, 2003.

8 Robert B. Marks, *Tigers, Rice, Silk and Silt: Environment and Economy in Late Imperial South China*. Cambridge: Cambridge University Press, 1998.

9   John Opie, *Ogallala: Water for a Dry Land*. Lincoln: University of Nebraska Press, 1993.
10 Donald Worster, "Doing Environmental History," p. 293.
11 Roderick Nash, *Wilderness and the American Mind*. Third edition. New Haven, CT: Yale University Press, 1982.
12 J. Donald Hughes, *North American Indian Ecology*. El Paso, TX: Texas Western Press, 1996.
13 John R. McNeill, "Observations on the Nature and Culture of Environmental History," *History and Theory* 42 (December 2003): 5–43. The quotation is on p. 9.
14 Donald Worster, "Doing Environmental History," p. 293.
15 J. M. Powell, *Historical Geography and Environmental History: An Australian Interface*, Clayton: Monash University Department of Geography and Environmental Science, Working Paper No. 40, 1995.
16 William A. Green, "Environmental History," in *History, Historians, and the Dynamics of Change*, by William A. Green. Westport, CT: Praeger, 1993, pp. 167–90.
17 Stephen Dovers, "Australian Environmental History: Introduction, Reviews and Principles," in *Australian Environmental History: Essays and Cases*, edited by Stephen Dovers, pp. 1–20. The quotation is on p. 7.
18 Ian Gordon Simmons, *Changing the Face of the Earth: Culture, Environment, History*. Oxford: Blackwell, 1989.
19 Ian Gordon Simmons, *Environmental History: A Concise Introduction*. Oxford: Blackwell, 1993.
20 Andrew Goudie, *The Human Impact on the Natural Environment*. Cambridge, MA: MIT Press, 2000.
21 Riley E. Dunlap, "Paradigmatic Change in Social Science: From Human Exemptions to an Ecological Paradigm," *American Behavioral Scientist* 24, 1 (September 1980): 5–14. The quotation is on p. 5.
22 William R. Catton, Jr. and Riley E. Dunlap, "A New Ecological Paradigm for Post-Exuberant Sociology," *American Behavioral Scientist* 24, 1 (September 1980): 15–47.
23 John Rodman, "Paradigm Change in Political Science: An Ecological Perspective," *American Behavioral Scientist* 24, 1 (September 1980): 49–78.
24 Herman E. Daly, "Growth Economics and the Fallacy of Misplaced Concreteness: Some Embarrassing Anomalies and an Emerging Steady-State Paradigm," *American Behavioral Scientist* 24, 1 (September 1980): 79–105.
25 Donald L. Hardesty, "The Ecological Perspective in Anthropology," *American Behavioral Scientist* 24, 1 (September 1980): 107–24.

26 McNeill, *Plagues and Peoples.*
27 Crosby, *The Columbian Exchange.*
28 Samuel P. Hays, *A History of Environmental Politics since 1945.* Pittsburgh, PA: University of Pittsburgh Press, 2000.
29 Clarence J. Glacken, *Traces on the Rhodian Shore: Nature and Culture in Western Thought from Ancient Times to the End of the Eighteenth Century.* Berkeley and Los Angeles, CA: University of California Press, 1967.
30 Lynn White, "The Historical Roots of Our Ecologic Crisis." *Science* 155 (1967): 1203–7.
31 Emmanuel Le Roy Ladurie, *Times of Feast, Times of Famine: A History of Climate since the Year 1000.* New York: Doubleday, 1971.
32 See, for example, H. H. Lamb, *Climate, History and the Modern World.* London: Routledge, 1995.
33 Christian Pfister, *500 Jahre Klimavariationen und Naturkatastrophen 1496–1996.* Bern: Paul Haput, 1999.
34 Richard Grove and John Chappell (eds), *El Niño, History and Crisis: Studies from the Asia-Pacific Region.* Cambridge: White Horse Press, 2000.
35 For information on this example, see Brent D. Shaw, "Climate, Environment, and History: The Case of Roman North Africa," in *Climate and History: Studies in Past Climates and Their Impact on Man,* edited by T. M. L. Wigley, M. J. Ingram, and G. Farmer. Cambridge: Cambridge University Press, 1981.
36 Paul B. Sears, "Ecology – A Subversive Subject," *BioScience* 14, 7 (July 1964): 11–13. The quotation is on p. 11.
37 Paul Shepard and Daniel McKinley (eds), *The Subversive Science: Essays Toward an Ecology of Man,* Boston, Houghton Mifflin, 1969.
38 Paul Shepard, "Introduction: Ecology and Man – A Viewpoint," in ibid., 1–10. The quotation is on p. 7.
39 Victor E. Shelford, *Laboratory and Field Ecology,* Baltimore, MD: Williams and Wilkins, 1929, p. 608.
40 Aldo Leopold, "Wilderness" (undated fragment), Leopold Papers 10–16, 16 (1935). Quoted in Curt Meine, *Aldo Leopold: His Life and Work,* Madison, WI: University of Wisconsin Press, 1988, pp. 359–60.
41 This idea is found in Roderick Nash, "Rounding Out the American Revolution: Ethical Extension and the New Environmentalism," in *Deep Ecology,* edited by Michael Tobias. San Diego, CA: Avant Books, 1985.
42 Douglas R. Weiner, "A Death-Defying Attempt to Articulate a Coherent Definition of Environmental History,"

Environmental History 10, 3 (July 2005): 404–20. The quotation is on p. 409.

43 Weiner bases the Indian example on Mike Davis, *Late Victorian Holocausts: El Niño Famines and the Making of the Third World*. London: Verso, 2001.

44 Mark David Spence, *Dispossessing the Wilderness: Indian Removal and the Making of the National Parks*. New York: Oxford University Press.

Chapter 2   Forerunners of Environmental History

1 Herodotus, *The Histories*, 1. 174, translated by Aubrey de Sélincourt. Harmondsworth: Penguin Books, 1972.

2 Ibid., 6. 75–80.

3 Thucydides, *History of the Peloponnesian War*, 1. 2, translated by Rex Warner. Harmondsworth: Penguin Books, 1972.

4 Ibid., 4. 108.

5 Ibid., 4. 3, 11 (Pylos); 6. 90 (Alcibiades).

6 Plato, *Critias*, 111, translated by Desmond Lee. Harmondsworth: Penguin Books, 1977.

7 Albert F. Verwilghen, *Mencius: The Man and His Ideas*, New York, St. John's University Press, 1967.

8 Mencius 6. A. 8. Quotations from Mencius, unless otherwise noted, are from the translation by D. C. Lau, *Mencius*, London, Penguin Books, 1970. This passage is on pp. 164–5.

9 Philip J. Ivanhoe, "Early Confucianism and Environmental Ethics," in *Confucianism and Ecology: The Interrelation of Heaven, Earth, and Humans*, edited by Mary Evelyn Tucker and John Berthrong, Cambridge, MA: Harvard University Press, 1998, pp. 59–76, see pp. 68–9.

10 Mencius 7. A. 24, p. 187.

11 Ibid., 4. A. 1, p. 118; 4. A. 14, p. 124.

12 Ibid., 6. B. 7, p. 176.

13 Xenophon, *Oeconomicus* 4. 8–9.

14 Herrlee Glessner Creel, *Chinese Thought from Confucius to Mao Tse-tung*, Chicago: University of Chicago Press, 1971, p. 82.

15 Mencius 7. B. 14, p. 196.

16 Ibid., 3. B. 3, p. 108.

17 Ibid., 2. A. 1, p. 85.

18 Ibid., 1. A. 3, p. 51. See also 7. A. 22, p. 186, which repeats another part of the same passage with small variations.

19 Ibid., 7. B. 34, p. 201; 1. B. 9, p. 68.
20 Creel, *Chinese Thought from Confucius to Mao Tse-tung*, p. 82.
21 Cicero, *De Natura Deorum* 2. 60, translated by H. Rackham. Cambridge, MA: Harvard University Press, 1951.
22 Ibn Khaldûn, *The Muqaddimah: An Introduction to History*, translated by Franz Rosenthal. New York: Pantheon Books, Bollingen Series 43, 1958.
23 Ibid., pp. 252–7.
24 Ibid., p. 308.
25 Clarence J. Glacken, *Traces on the Rhodian Shore*. Berkeley and Los Angeles, CA: University of California Press, 1967, pp. 213–14, 349–50.
26 Ibid., pp. 259–61.
27 Charles R. Young, *The Royal Forests of Medieval England*. Philadelphia, PA: University of Pennsylvania Press, 1979, pp. 2–3. Quoted from *The Anglo-Saxon Chronicle*, edited by Dorothy Whitelock, New Brunswick, NJ: Rutgers University Press, 1961, p. 165.
28 Ronald E. Zupko and Robert A. Laures, *Straws in the Wind: Medieval Urban Environmental Law, The Case of Northern Italy*. Boulder, CO: Westview Press, 1996.
29 Richard H. Grove, *Green Imperialism: Colonial Expansion, Tropical Island Edens and the Origins of Environmentalism, 1600–1860*. Cambridge: Cambridge University Press, 1995.
30 Richard H. Grove, "Origins of Western Environmentalism," *Scientific American* 267, 1 (July 1992): 42–7.
31 Grove, *Green Imperialism*, p. 221.
32 Ibid., pp. 203, 206.
33 Ibid., p. 371.
34 George Perkins Marsh, *Man and Nature*, 1864. Edited by David Lowenthal. Cambridge, MA: The Belknap Press of Harvard University Press, 1965.
35 Ibid., pp. 10–11.
36 Ibid., p. 52.
37 Ibid., p. 43.
38 Ibid., p. 15.
39 Peter Burke, *The French Historical Revolution: The Annales School, 1929–89*. Stanford, CA: Stanford University Press, 1990. This book is a study of this group and is valuable for the student, although Burke does not discuss the connection with environmental history.
40 Lucien Febvre, *A Geographical Introduction to History*. New York: Alfred A. Knopf, 1925.

41 Ibid., p. 85.
42 Ibid., p. 171.
43 Ibid., p. 355.
44 Ibid., p. 288.
45 Fernand Braudel, *The Mediterranean and the Mediterranean World in the Age of Philip II*. First edition, 1949, second edition, 1966, translated by Siân Reynolds. New York: Harper & Row, 1972.
46 Ibid., p. 25.
47 Ibid., p. 142.
48 Ibid., p. 239.
49 Ibid., p. 268.
50 Emmanuel Le Roy Ladurie, *Times of Feast, Times of Famine: A History of Climate since the Year 1000*. French edition, 1967. Garden City, NY: Doubleday, 1971.
51 Frederick Jackson Turner, "The Significance of the Frontier in American History," American Historical Association, *Annual Report for the Year 1893*. Washington, DC: AHA, 1893, pp. 199–227.
52 Walter Prescott Webb, "Geographical-Historical Concepts in American History," *Annals of the Association of American Geographers* 50 (1960): 85–93.
53 James C. Malin, *The Grassland of North America: Prolegomena to Its History*. 1947. Reprint. Gloucester, MA: Peter Smith, 1967.

Chapter 3   The Birth and Growth of Environmental History in the United States

1 J. R. McNeill, "Observations on the Nature and Culture of Environmental History," *History and Theory, Theme Issue* 42 (December 2003): 5–43.
2 Ibid., p. 5.
3 Stewart Udall, *The Quiet Crisis*. New York: Holt, Rinehart and Winston, 1963. This book was revised and reissued 25 years later as *The Quiet Crisis and the Next Generation*. Salt Lake City, UT: Peregrine Smith, 1988.
4 Samuel P. Hays, *Conservation and the Gospel of Efficiency*. Cambridge: Cambridge University Press, 1959.
5 Adam Rome, "Conservation, Preservation, and Environmental Activism: A Survey of the Historical Literature." National Park Service website, "History: Links to the Past." <www.cr.nps.gov/history/hisnps/NPSThinking/nps-oah.htm>.

6 Roderick Nash, *Wilderness and the American Mind*. New Haven, CT: Yale University Press, 1967.

7 Samuel Hays, "From Conservation to Environment: Environmental Politics in the United States Since World War II," *Environmental Review* 6, 2 (1982): 14–41; Samuel Hays, *Beauty, Health, and Permanence: Environmental Politics in the United States, 1955–1985*. Cambridge: Cambridge University Press, 1987.

8 John Opie, "Environmental History: Pitfalls and Opportunities," *Environmental Review* 7, 1 (Spring 1983): 8–16.

9 Richard White, "American Environmental History: The Development of a New Historical Field," *Pacific Historical Review* 54 (August 1985): 297–337. See also a retrospective piece by the same author, "Afterword, Environmental History: Watching a Historical Field Mature," *Pacific Historical Review* 70 (February 2001): 103–11.

10 Carolyn Merchant, *The Columbia Guide to American Environmental History*. New York: Columbia University Press, 2002.

11 Alfred Crosby, *The Columbian Exchange: Biological and Cultural Consequences of 1492*. Westport, CT: Greenwood Press, 1972. Republication with new material, Westport, CT: Praeger Publishers, 2003.

12 Calvin Luther Martin, *Keepers of the Game: Indian–Animal Relationships and the Fur Trade*. Berkeley and Los Angeles, CA: University of California Press, 1978.

13 Joseph M. Petulla, *American Environmental History*. Columbus, OH: Merrill Publishing, 1988. First edition, 1977, Boyd & Fraser.

14 John Opie, *Nature's Nation: An Environmental History of the United States*. Fort Worth, TX: Harcourt Brace, 1998.

15 Ted Steinberg, *Down to Earth: Nature's Role in American History*. New York: Oxford University Press, 2002.

16 Walter Prescott Webb, *The Great Plains*. Boston: Ginn and Company, 1931; James C. Malin, *The Grassland of North America: Prolegomena to Its History*. First edition, 1947. Reprint. Gloucester, MA: Peter Smith, 1967.

17 Wilbur R. Jacobs, "Frontiersmen, Fur Traders, and Other Varmints: An Ecological Appraisal of the Frontier in American History," *AHA Newsletter* (November 1970): 5–11.

18 Donald Worster, *Dust Bowl: The Southern Plains in the 1930s*. New York: Oxford University Press, 1979. Paul Bonnifield: *The Dust Bowl: Men, Dirt, and Depression*. Albuquerque: University of New Mexico Press, 1979. For a

comparative review of these books, see William Cronon, "A Place for Stories: Nature, History, and Narrative," *Journal of American History* 78, 4 (March 1992): 1347–76.

19   Andrew Isenberg, *The Destruction of the Bison: Social and Ecological Changes in the Great Plains, 1750–1920.* Chapel Hill, NC: University of North Carolina Press, 2000.

20   Carolyn Merchant (ed.), *Green versus Gold: Sources in California's Environmental History.* Washington, DC: Island Press, 1998.

21   William Cronon, *Changes in the Land: Indians, Colonists, and the Ecology of New England.* New York: Hill and Wang, 1983.

22   Carolyn Merchant, *Ecological Revolutions: Nature, Gender, and Science in New England.* Chapel Hill, NC: University of North Carolina Press, 1989.

23   Richard W. Judd, *Common Lands, Common People: The Origins of Conservation in Northern New England.* Cambridge, MA: Harvard University Press, 1997.

24   Albert E. Cowdrey, *This Land, This South: An Environmental History.* Lexington, KT: University of Kentucky Press, 1983.

25   Carville Earle, "The Myth of the Southern Soil Miner: Macrohistory, Agricultural Innovation, and Environmental Change," in *The Ends of the Earth*, edited by Donald Worster. Cambridge: Cambridge University Press, 1988, pp. 175–210.

26   Otis Graham, "Again the Backward Region? Environmental History in and of the American South," *Southern Cultures* 6, 2 (2000).

27   David Lowenthal, *George Perkins Marsh, Prophet of Conservation.* Seattle, WA: University of Washington Press, 2000. This is a revised edition of David Lowenthal, *George Perkins Marsh: Versatile Vermonter.* New York: Columbia University Press, 1958.

28   Stephen R. Fox, *John Muir and His Legacy: The American Conservation Movement.* Boston: Little, Brown, 1981; Michael P. Cohen, *The Pathless Way: John Muir and American Wilderness.* Madison, WI: University of Wisconsin Press, 1984; Thurman Wilkins, *John Muir: Apostle of Nature.* Norman, OK: University of Oklahoma Press, 1995.

29   Steven J. Holmes, *The Young John Muir: An Environmental Biography.* Madison, WI: University of Wisconsin Press, 1999.

30   Harold T. Pinkett, *Gifford Pinchot: Private and Public Forester.* Chicago: University of Illinois Press, 1970; Char Miller,

Gifford Pinchot and the Making of Modern Environmentalism. Washington, DC: Island Press, 2001.

31 W. Todd Benson, *President Theodore Roosevelt's Conservation Legacy*. Consohocken, PA: Infinity Publishing, 2003; Paul Russell Cutright, *Theodore Roosevelt: The Making of a Conservationist*. Urbana, IL: University of Illinois Press, 1985; A. L. Riesch-Owen, *Conservation under FDR*. New York: Prager, 1983.

32 Susan L. Flader, *Thinking Like a Mountain: Aldo Leopold and the Evolution of an Ecological Attitude toward Deer, Wolves, and Forests*. Madison, WI: University of Wisconsin Press, 1994.

33 Linda Lear, *Rachel Carson: Witness for Nature*. New York: Henry Holt, 1997.

34 Harold K. Steen, *The U.S. Forest Service: A History*. Seattle: University of Washington Press, 1976; Paul W. Hirt, *A Conspiracy of Optimism: Management of the National Forests since World War II*. Lincoln, NE: University of Nebraska Press, 1994.

35 Alfred Runte, *National Parks: The American Experience*. Lincoln, NE: University of Nebraska Press, 1979; Richard W. Sellars, *Preserving Nature in the National Parks*. New Haven, CT: Yale University Press, 1997.

36 In 2004, the NCPH and ASEH held a joint conference in Victoria, Canada, which attracted more than 700 participants.

37 See, for example, Richard J. Lazarus, *The Making of Environmental Law*. Chicago: University of Chicago Press, 2004.

38 Michael P. Cohen, *The History of the Sierra Club, 1892–1970*. San Francisco: Sierra Club Books, 1988.

39 Byron E. Pearson, *Still the Wild River Runs: Congress, the Sierra Club, and the Fight to Save the Grand Canyon*. Tucson, AZ: University of Arizona Press, 2002.

40 Martin V. Melosi, *Garbage in the Cities: Refuse, Reform, and the Environment, 1880–1980*. Pittsburgh, PA: University of Pittsburgh Press, 2005. Reprint of 1981 edition; *The Sanitary City: Urban Infrastructure in America from Colonial Times to the Present*. Akron, OH: Akron University Press, 1996; *Effluent America: Cities, Industry, Energy, and the Environment*. Pittsburgh, PA: University of Pittsburgh Press, 2001.

41 Joel Tarr, *The Search for the Ultimate Sink: Urban Pollution in Historical Perspective*. Akron, OH: Akron University Press, 1996.

42 Mike Davis, *The Ecology of Fear: Los Angeles and the Imagination of Disaster*. New York: Metropolitan Books, 1998; Ari Kelman, *A River and Its City: The Nature of Landscape in New Orleans*. Berkeley and Los Angeles, CA: University of California Press, 2003.

43 Martin V. Melosi, "Equity, Eco-Racism, and the Environmental Justice Movement," in *The Face of the Earth*, edited by J. Donald Hughes. Armonk, NY and London: M. E. Sharpe, 2000, pp. 47–75.

44 Robert D. Bullard (ed.), *Unequal Protection: Environmental Justice and Communities of Color*. San Francisco: Sierra Club Books, 1994.

45 Carolyn Merchant, *Earthcare: Women and the Environment*. New York: Routledge, 1995. See also Carolyn Merchant, *The Death of Nature: Women, Ecology, and the Scientific Revolution*. New York: Harper and Row, 1980.

46 Susan R. Schrepfer, *Nature's Altars: Mountains, Gender and American Environmentalism*. Lawrence, KS: University Press of Kansas, 2005; Jennifer Price, *Flight Maps: Adventures with Nature in Modern America*. Cambridge, MA: Basic Books, 2000.

47 Elizabeth D. Blum, "Linking American Women's History and Environmental History: A Preliminary Historiography." ASEH website, available as of August, 2005 at <www.h-net.org/~environ/historiography/uswomen.htm>.

48 *Environmental History*, published in Durham, North Carolina.

49 Jeffrey K. Stine and Joel A. Tarr, "At the Intersection of Histories: Technology and the Environment," *Technology and Culture* 39, 4 (1998): 601–40.

50 Carroll Pursell, *The Machine in America: A Social History of Technology*. Baltimore, MD: Johns Hopkins University Press, 1995.

51 Martin V. Melosi, *Garbage in the Cities; Coping with Abundance: Energy and Environment in Industrial America*. Philadelphia, PA: Temple University Press, 1985.

52 As of 2005, the URL is <www.udel.edu/History/gpetrick/envirotech>.

53 Alfred W. Crosby, "The Past and Present of Environmental History," *American Historical Review* 100, 4 (October 1995): 1177–89.

54 Donald Worster, "Arranging a Marriage: Ecology and Agriculture," Chapter 5 in *The Wealth of Nature: Environmental History and the Ecological Imagination*. New York: Oxford

University Press, 1993, pp. 64–70; also in *Major Problems in American Environmental History: Documents and Essays*, edited by Carolyn Merchant. Lexington, MA: D. C. Heath, 1993.

55 Mart A. Stewart, "If John Muir Had Been an Agrarian: American Environmental History West and South," *Environment and History* 11, 2 (May 2005): 139–62.

56 Michael Williams, *Deforesting the Earth: From Prehistory to Global Crisis*. Chicago: University of Chicago Press, 2003, p. 5.

57 Harold K. Steen, *The Forest History Society and Its History*. Durham, NC: Forest History Society, 1996.

58 Michael Williams, *Americans and Their Forests: A Historical Geography*. Cambridge: Cambridge University Press, 1992; Thomas R. Cox, Robert S. Maxwell, and Philip D. Thomas (eds), *This Well-Wooded Land: Americans and Their Forests from Colonial Times to the Present*. Lincoln, NE: University of Nebraska Press, 1985.

59 Harold K. Steen, *Forest and Wildlife Science in America: A History*. Durham, NC: Forest History Society, 1999.

60 Richard Grove, "Environmental History," in *New Perspectives in Historical Writing*, edited by Peter Burke. Cambridge: Polity, 2001, pp. 261–82.

61 Thomas R. Dunlap, *Nature and the English Diaspora: Environment and History in the United States, Canada, Australia, and New Zealand*. Cambridge: Cambridge University Press, 1999.

62 Marcus Hall, *Earth Repair: A Transatlantic History of Environmental Restoration*. Charlottesville, VA: University of Virginia Press, 2005.

Chapter 4 Local, Regional, and National Environmental Histories

1 J. Donald Hughes, "Environmental History – World," in *A Global Encyclopedia of Historical Writing*, 2 vols., edited by David R. Woolf, New York, Garland Publishing, 1998, Vol. 1, 288–91.

2 For articles and inclusive bibliography, see the *Indonesian Environmental History Newsletter*, 12, June 1999, published by EDEN (Ecology, Demography and Economy in Nusantara), KITLV (Koningklijk Institut voor Taal-, Land- en Volkenkunde, Royal Institute of Linguistics and

Anthropology), PO Box 9515, 2300 RA Leiden, Netherlands.

3 Tim Flannery, *The Future Eaters: An Ecological History of the Australasian Lands and People*. New York: George Braziller, 1995.

4 Tim Flannery, *The Eternal Frontier: An Ecological History of North America and Its Peoples*. New York: Atlantic Monthly Press, 2001.

5 Madhav Gadgil and Ramachandra Guha, *This Fissured Land: An Ecological History of India*. Berkeley and Los Angeles, CA: University of California Press, 1992.

6 Donald Worster, "World Without Borders: The Internationalizing of Environmental History." *Environmental Review* 6, 2 (Fall 1982): 8–13.

7 Twenty-seven and eleven, if Worster's address is counted. Kendall E. Bailes (ed.), *Environmental History: Critical Issues in Comparative Perspective*. Lanham, MD: University Press of America, 1985.

8 *Environmental Review* 8, 3 (Fall 1984).

9 Peter Coates, "Emerging from the Wilderness (or, from Redwoods to Bananas): Recent Environmental History in the United States and the Rest of the Americas," *Environment and History* 10, 4 (November 2004): 407–38, especially "Of Mice (Beaver?) and Elephants: Canada and North American Environmental History," pp. 421–3.

10 Graeme Wynn and Matthew Evenden, "Fifty-four, Forty, or Fight? Writing Within and Across Boundaries in North American Environmental History," paper presented at a conference on "The Uses of Environmental History" at the Centre for History and Economics, University of Cambridge, UK, January 13–14, 2006.

11 Graeme Wynn, guest editor, "On the Environment," *BC Studies* 142/3 (Summer/Autumn 2004).

12 Theodore Binnema, *Common and Contested Ground: A Human and Environmental History of the Northwest Plains*. Norman, OK: University of Oklahoma Press, 2001; Douglas Harris, *Fish, Law and Colonialism: The Legal Capture of Salmon in British Columbia*. Toronto: University of Toronto Press, 2001; Arthur J. Ray, "Diffusion of Diseases in the Western Interior of Canada, 1830–1850," *Geographical Review* 66 (1976), 156–81; Jody F. Decker, "Country Distempers: Deciphering Disease and Illness in Rupert's Land before 1870," in Jennifer Brown and Elizabeth Vibert (eds), *Reading Beyond Words: Documenting Native History*. Calgary: Broadview Press, 1996; Mary-Ellen Kelm, "British

Columbia's First Nations and the Influenza Pandemic of 1918–1919," *BC Studies* 122 (1999): 23–48.

13 Neil Forkey, *Shaping the Upper Canadian Frontier: Environment, Society, and Culture in the Trent Valley.* Calgary: University of Calgary Press, 2003; Matthew Hatvany, *Marshlands: Four Centuries of Environmental Changes on the Shores of the St. Lawrence.* Sainte-Foy: Les Presses de l'Université Laval, 2004; Clint Evans, *The War on Weeds in the Prairie West: An Environmental History.* Calgary: University of Calgary Press, 2002.

14 Richard Rajala, *Clearcutting the Pacific Rain Forest.* Vancouver: University of British Columbia Press, 1998; Jean Manore, *Cross-Currents: Hydroelectricity and the Engineering of Northern Ontario.* Waterloo: Wilfred Laurier Press, 1999; Matthew Evenden, *Fish versus Power: An Environmental History of the Fraser River.* Cambridge: Cambridge University Press, 2004.

15 Tina Loo, "Making a Modern Wilderness: Wildlife Management in Canada, 1900–1950," *Canadian Historical Review* 82 (2001): 91–121; John Sandlos, "From the Outside Looking In: Aesthetics, Politics and Wildlife Conservation in the Canadian North," *Environmental History* 6, 1 (2001): 6–31; Kurkpatrick Dorsey, *The Dawn of Conservation Diplomacy: US – Canadian Wildlife Protection Treaties in the Progressive Era.* Seattle: University of Washington Press, 1998.

16 Suzanne Zeller, *Inventing Canada: Early Victorian Science and the Idea of a Transcontinental Nation.* Toronto: University of Toronto Press, 1987; Stephen Bocking, *Ecologists and Environmental Politics: A History of Contemporary Ecology.* New Haven, CT: Yale University Press, 1997; Stéphane Castonguay, *Protection des cultures, construction de la nature: L'entomologie économique au Canada.* Saint-Nicolas: Septentrion, 2004.

17 Michelle Dagenais, "Fuir la ville: villégiature et villégiatures dans la région de Montréal, 1890–1940," *Revue d'histoire de l'Amérique française* 58, 3 (Spring 2005): 1–27.

18 Stephen Bocking, guest ed., "The Nature of Cities," special issue of *Urban History Review* 34, 1 (Fall 2005).

19 Ken Cruikshank and Nancy B. Bouchier, "Blighted Areas and Obnoxious Industries: Constructing Environmental Inequality on an Industrial Waterfront, Hamilton, Ontario, 1890–1960," *Environmental History* 9 (2004): 464–96.

20 Cate Sandilands, "Where the Mountain Men Meet the Lesbian Rangers: Gender, Nation, and Nature in the Rocky Mountain National Parks," in Melody Hessing, Rebecca

Ragion, and Catriona Sandilands (eds), *This Elusive Country: Women and the Canadian Environment*. Vancouver: UBC Press, 2004; Tina Loo, "Of Moose and Men: Hunting for Masculinities in the Far West," *Western Historical Quarterly* 32 (2001): 296–319.

21   Richard Charles Hoffmann, *Fishers' Craft and Lettered Art: Tracts on Fishing from the End of the Middle Ages*. Toronto: University of Toronto Press, 1997; and *Land, Liberties and Lordship in a Late Medieval Countryside: Agrarian Structures and Change in the Duchy of Wroclaw*. Philadelphia, PA: University of Pennsylvania Press, 1989.

22   Verena Winiwarter (ed.), Marco Armiero, Petra van Dam, Andreas Dix, Per Eliasson, Poul Holm, Leoš Jeleček, Robert A. Lambert, Geneviève Massard-Guilbaud, Manuel Gonzales de Molina, Timo Myllyntaus, Jan Oosthoek, Christian Pfister, and Lajos Rácz, "Environmental History in Europe from 1994 to 2004: Enthusiasm and Consolidation," *Environment and History* 10, 4 (November 2004): 501–30.

23   Mark Cioc, Björn-Ola Linnér, and Matt Osborn, "Environmental History Writing in Northern Europe," *Environmental History* 5, 3 (July 2000): 396–406.

24   Leoš Jeleček, Pavel Chromy, Helena Janu, Josef Miskovsky, and Lenka Uhlirova (eds), *Dealing with Diversity*. Prague: Charles University in Prague, Faculty of Science, 2003; Mauro Agnoletti, Marco Armiero, Stefania Barca, and Gabriella Corona (eds), *History and Sustainability*. Florence: University of Florence, Dipartimento di Scienze e Tecnologie Ambientali e Forestali, 2005.

25   Peter Brimblecombe and Christian Pfister, *The Silent Countdown: Essays in European Environmental History*. Berlin: Springer-Verlag, 1990.

26   Timo Myllyntaus and Mikko Saikku (eds), *Encountering the Past in Nature*. Athens, OH: Ohio University Press, 2001.

27   Matt Osborn, "Sowing the Field of British Environmental History," 2001, available at this writing (2005) at <www.h-net.org/~environ/historiography/british.htm>.

28   W. G. Hoskins, *The Making of the English Landscape*. London: Hodder and Stoughton, ([1955] 1977).

29   H. C. Darby, *A New Historical Geography of England*. 2 vols: *Before 1600; After 1600*. Cambridge: Cambridge University Press, 1973 and 1976.

30   I. G. Simmons, *An Environmental History of Great Britain: From 10,000 Years Ago to the Present*. Edinburgh: Edinburgh University Press, 2001.

31   Keith Thomas, *Man and the Natural World: Changing Attitudes in England 1500–1800*. London: Allan Lane, 1983.

32   John Sheail, *An Environmental History of Twentieth-Century Britain*. New York: Palgrave, 2002.

33   Oliver Rackham, *An Illustrated History of the Countryside*. London: Weidenfeld and Nicolson, 2003; by the same author, *Trees and Woodland in the British Landscape: A Complete History of Britain's Trees, Woods and Hedgerows*. London: Phoenix Press, 2001; and *The History of the Countryside*. London: J. M. Dent and Sons, 1993.

34   B. W. Clapp, *An Environmental History of Britain Since the Industrial Revolution*. London: Longman, 1994.

35   Peter Brimblecombe, *The Big Smoke: A History of Air Pollution in London Since Medieval Times*. London: Routledge and Kegan Paul, 1987.

36   Dale H. Porter, *The Thames Embankment: Environment, Technology, and Society in Victorian London*. Akron, OH: University of Akron Press, 1998.

37   T. C. Smout, *Nature Contested: Environmental History in Scotland and Northern England since 1600*. Edinburgh: Edinburgh University Press, 2000; T. C. Smout, *People and Woods in Scotland: A History*. Edinburgh: Edinburgh University Press, 2003. See also his edited volumes, *Scotland Since Prehistory: Natural Change and Human Impact*. Aberdeen: Scottish Cultural Press, 1993; and (with R. A. Lambert), *Rothiemurchus: Nature and People on a Highland Estate 1500–2000*. Edinburgh: Scottish Cultural Press, 1999.

38   Fiona Watson, *Scotland: From Prehistory to Present*. Stroud: Tempus Publishing, 2003.

39   T. C. Smout, Alan R. MacDonald, and Fiona J. Watson, *A History of the Native Woodlands of Scotland, 1520–1920*. Edinburgh: Edinburgh University Press, 2005.

40   *Annales* 29, 3, 1993.

41   Pascal Acot, *Histoire de l'écologie*. Paris: Presses Universitaires de France, 1988; J. M. Drouin, *Réinventer la nature: l'écologie et son histoire*. Paris: Desclée de Brower, 1991.

42   Françoise d'Eaubonne, *Le féminisme ou la mort (Feminism or Death!)*. Paris: Horay, 1974.

43   Joseph Szarka, *The Shaping of Environmental Policy in France*. New York: Berghahn Books, 2002; Emile Leynaud, *L'Etat et la Nature: l'exemple des parcs nationaux français*. Florac: Parc National des Cévennes, 1985.

44   Andrée Corvol, *L'Homme aux bois: Histoire des relations de l'homme et de la forêt, XVIIIe–XXe siècles (Man in the*

Woods: A History of Human–Forest Relations, Eighteenth to the Twentieth Centuries). Paris: Fayard, 1987; Louis Badré, *Histoire de la forêt française (History of the French Forest).* Paris: Les Éditions Arthaud, 1983.

45 R. Neboit-Guilhot and L. Davy, *Les français dans leur environnement.* Paris: Nathan, 1996.

46 Michael Bess, *The Light-Green Society: Ecology and Technological Modernity in France, 1960–2000.* Chicago: University of Chicago Press, 2004.

47 Christoph Bernhardt and Geneviève Massard-Guilbaud (eds), *Le Démon moderne: La pollution dans les sociétés urbaines et industrielles d'Europe (The Modern Demon: Pollution in Urban and Industrial European Societies).* Clermont-Ferrand: Presses Universitaires Blaise-Pascal, 2002; and Dieter Schott, Bill Luckin and Geneviève Massard-Guilbaud (eds), *Resources of the City: Contributions to an Environmental History of Modern Europe.* Aldershot: Ashgate, 2005.

48 Verena Winiwarter, *Umweltgeschichte: Eine Einführung (Environmental History: An Introduction).* Stuttgart: UTB, 2005.

49 Christian Pfister, *Wetternachhersage: 500 Jahre Klimavariationen und Naturkatastrophen, 1496–1995 (Evidence of Past Weather: 500 Years of Climatic Variations and Natural Catastrophes, 1496–1995).* Bern: P. Haupt, 1999.

50 Joachim Radkau, *Natur und Macht (Nature and Power).* Munich: C. H. Beck, 2000.

51 Joachim Radkau and Frank Uekötter, *Naturschutz und Nationalsozialismus (Nature Protection and National Socialism).* Berlin: Campus Fachbuch, 2003.

52 Anna Bramwell, *Blood and Soil: Richard Walther Darré and Hitler's "Green Party."* Abbotsbrook, Bourne End, Buckinghamshire: Kensal Press, 1985.

53 Mark Cioc, "Germany," in *Encyclopedia of World Environmental History*, edited by Shepard Krech III, J. R. McNeill, and Carolyn Merchant. New York: Routledge, 2004. 3 vols. Vol. 3, p. 586.

54 Mark Cioc, *The Rhine: An Eco-Biography, 1815–2000.* Seattle, WA: University of Washington Press, 2002.

55 Raymond H. Dominick, *The Environmental Movement in Germany: Prophets and Pioneers, 1871–1971.* Bloomington, IN: Indiana University Press, 1992.

56 Markus Klein and Jürgen W. Falter, *Der lange Weg der Grünen (The Long Path of the Greens).* Munich: C. H. Beck, 2003.

57 G. P. van de Ven, *Man-Made Lowlands: History of Water Management and Land Reclamation in the Netherlands.* Utrecht: Uitgeverij Matrijs, 1993.

58 Henny J. van der Windt, *En Dan, Wat Is Natuur Nog in Dit Land?: Natuurbescherming in Nederland 1880–1990 (And What Then, What Is Still Nature in This Country?: Nature Conservation in the Netherlands, 1880–1990).* Amsterdam: Boom, 1995.

59 *Jaarboek voor Ecologische Geschiednis*, Ghent/Hilversum: Academia Press and Verloren.

60 Petra J. E. M. van Dam, *Vissen in Veenmeeren: De sluisvisserij op aal tussen Haarlem en Amsterdam en de ecologische transformatie in Rijnland, 1440–1530.* Hilversum: Verloren, 1998.

61 William H. TeBrake, *Medieval Frontier: Culture and Ecology in Rijnland.* College Station, TX: Texas A&M University Press, 1984.

62 Andrew Jamison, Ron Eyerman, and Jacqueline Cramer, *The Making of the New Environmental Consciousness: A Comparative Study of the Environmental Movements in Sweden, Denmark and the Netherlands.* Edinburgh: Edinburgh University Press, 1990.

63 Timo Myllyntaus, "Writing about the Past with Green Ink: The Emergence of Finnish Environmental History." Available at this writing (2005) at <www.h-net.org/~environ/historiography/finland.htm>; also in *Skrifter fran forskningsprogrammet Landskapet som arena nr X*, edited by Erland Marald and Christer Nordlund. Umeå: Umeå University, 2003.

64 Yrjö Haila and Richard Levins, *Humanity and Nature: Ecology, Science and Society.* London: LPC Group, 1992.

65 For example, Jussi Raumolin, *The Problem of Forest-Based Development as Illustrated by the Development Discussion, 1850–1918.* Helsinki: University of Helsinki, Department of Social Policy, 1990.

66 Simo Laakkonen, *Vesiensuojelun synty: Helsingin ja sen merialueen ympäristöühistoriaa 1878–1928 (The Origins of Water Protection in Helsinki, 1878–1928).* With English summary. Helsinki: Gaudeamus, 2001.

67 L. Anders Sandberg and Sverker Sörlin, *Sustainability, the Challenge: People, Power, and the Environment.* Vancouver: Black Rose Press, 1998.

68 Sverker Sörlin and Anders Öckerman. *Jorden en Ö: En Global Miljöhistoria (Earth an Island: A Global Environmental History).* Stockholm: Natur och Kultur, 1998.

69 Thorkild Kjærgaard, *The Danish Revolution, 1500–1800: An Ecohistorical Interpretation.* Trans. David Hohnen. Cambridge: Cambridge University Press, 1994.

70 Leos Jelecek, Pavel Chromy, Helena Janu, Josef Miskovsky, and Lenka Uhlirova (eds), *Dealing with Diversity: 2nd International Conference of the European Society for Environmental History Prague 2003.* 2 vols. (*Proceedings* and *Abstract Book*). Prague: Charles University in Prague, Faculty of Science, 2003.

71 Lajos Rácz, *Climate History of Hungary Since the 16th Century: Past, Present and Future.* Pécs: MTA RKK, 1999.

72 Jószef Laszlovszky and Peter Szabó (eds), *People and Nature in Historical Perspective.* Budapest: CEU Press, 2003.

73 Douglas R. Weiner, *Models of Nature: Ecology, Conservation, and Cultural Revolution in Soviet Russia.* Bloomington, IN: Indiana University Press, 1988. Second edition, 2000.

74 Douglas R. Weiner, *A Little Corner of Freedom: Russian Nature Protection from Stalin to Gorbachev.* Berkeley and Los Angeles, CA: University of California Press, 1999.

75 Douglas R. Weiner, "Russia and the Soviet Union," in *Encyclopedia of World Environmental History*, edited by Shepard Krech III, J. R. McNeill, and Carolyn Merchant. New York: Routledge, 2004. 3 vols. Vol. 3, pp. 1074–80.

76 John R. McNeill, *The Mountains of the Mediterranean World: An Environmental History.* Cambridge: Cambridge University Press, 1992. See also J. R. McNeill, "Mediterranean Sea," in *Encyclopedia of World Environmental History*, edited by Shepard Krech III, J. R. McNeill, and Carolyn Merchant. New York: Routledge, 2004. 3 vols. Vol. 2, pp. 826–8.

77 J. Donald Hughes, *The Mediterranean: An Environmental History.* Santa Barbara, CA: ABC-CLIO, 2005.

78 Alfred T. Grove and Oliver Rackham. *The Nature of Mediterranean Europe: An Ecological History.* New Haven, CT: Yale University Press, 2001.

79 Peregrine Horden and Nicholas Purcell, *The Corrupting Sea: A Study of Mediterranean History.* Oxford: Blackwell, 2000.

80 J. Donald Hughes, *Pan's Travail: Environmental Problems of the Ancient Greeks and Romans.* Baltimore, MD: Johns Hopkins University Press, 1994.

81 Manuel Gonzáles de Molina and J. Martínez-Alier, who edited a collection entitled *Naturaleza Transformada: Estudios de Historia Ambiental en España* (*Nature Transformed:*

Studies in Environmental History in Spain). Barcelona: Icaria, 2001.

82   Juan García Latorre, Andrés Sánchez Picón, and Jesús García Latorre, "The Man-Made Desert: Effects of Economic and Demographic Growth on the Ecosystems of Arid Southeastern Spain," *Environmental History* 6, 1 (January 2001): 75–94.

83   Alberto Vieira (ed.), *História e Meio-Ambiente: O Impacto da Expansão Europeia (History and Environment: The Impact of the European Expansion)*. Funchal, Madeira: Centro de Estudos de História do Atlântico, 1999.

84   Piero Bevilacqua, *La mucca è savia: Ragioni storiche della crisi alimentare europea (The Savvy Cow: History of the European Food Crisis)*. Rome: Donzelli, 2002.

85   Piero Bevilacqua, *Tra natura e storia: Ambiente, economie, risorse in Italia (Between Nature and History: Environment, Economy, and Resources in Italy)*. Rome: Donzelli, 1996.

86   Chloé A. Vlassopoulou, "Automobile Pollution: Agenda Denial vs. Agenda Setting in Early Century France and Greece," *History and Sustainability*, edited by Mauro Agnoletti, Marco Armiero, Stefania Barca, and Gabriella Corona, Florence: University of Florence, Dipartimento di Scienze e Tecnologie Ambientali e Forestali, 2005, pp. 252–6.

87   Alexis Franghiadis, "Commons and Change: The Case of the Greek 'National Estates' (19th–Early 20th Centuries);" Alexandra Yerolympos, "Fire Prevention and Planning in Mediterranean Cities, 1800–1920," *Dealing with Diversity, Abstract Book*, edited by Leos Jelecek, Pavel Chromy, Helena Janu, Josef Miskovsky, and Lenka Uhlirova, Prague: Charles University in Prague, Faculty of Science, 2003, pp. 55–6, 138–9.

88   Alon Tal, *Pollution in a Promised Land: An Environmental History of Israel*. Berkeley and Los Angeles, CA: University of California Press, 2002.

89   Madhav Gadgil and Ramachandra Guha, *This Fissured Land*.

90   David Arnold and Ramachandra Guha (eds), *Nature, Culture, Imperialism: Essays on the Environmental History of South Asia*. New Delhi: Oxford University Press, 1995.

91   Richard Grove, Vinita Damodaran, and Satpal Sangwan (eds), *Nature and the Orient: The Environmental History of South and Southeast Asia*. Delhi: Oxford University Press, 1998.

92   Ajay S. Rawat (ed.), *History of Forestry in India*. New Delhi: Indus Publishing, 1991; by the same author, *Indian Forestry: A Perspective*. New Delhi: Indus Publishing, 1993.

93 Ravi Rajan, *Modernizing Nature: Forestry and Imperial Eco-Development, 1800–1950*. Oxford: Oxford University Press, 2006.

94 Rana P. B. Singh (ed.), *The Spirit and Power of Place: Human Environment and Sacrality*. Banaras: National Geographical Society of India, 1993.

95 Madhav Gadgil and M. D. Subash Chandran, "On the History of Uttara Kannada Forests," in *Changing Tropical Forests*, edited by John Dargavel, Kay Dixon, and Noel Semple. Canberra: Centre for Resource and Environmental Studies, 1988, pp. 47–58. See also M. D. Subash Chandran and J. Donald Hughes, "Sacred Groves and Conservation: The Comparative History of Traditional Reserves in the Mediterranean Area and in South India," *Environment and History* 6, 2 (May 2000): 169–86.

96 Laxman D. Satya, *Ecology, Colonialism, and Cattle: Central India in the Nineteenth Century*. New Delhi: Oxford University Press, 2004.

97 Peter Boomgaard, *Frontiers of Fear: Tigers and People in the Malay World, 1600–1950*. New Haven, CT: Yale University Press, 2001.

98 Peter Boomgaard, Freek Colombijn, and David Henley (eds), *Paper Landscapes: Explorations in the Environmental History of Indonesia*. Leiden: KITLV Press, 1997.

99 Bao Maohong, "Environmental History in China," *Environment and History* 10, 4 (November 2004): 475–99.

100 Mark Elvin, *The Retreat of the Elephants: An Environmental History of China*. New Haven, CT: Yale University Press, 2004.

101 Mark Elvin and Liu Tsui-jung (eds), *Sediments of Time: Environment and Society in Chinese History*. Cambridge: Cambridge University Press, 1998.

102 Judith Shapiro, *Mao's War against Nature: Politics and the Environment in Revolutionary China*. Cambridge: Cambridge University Press, 2001.

103 Robert B. Marks, *Tigers, Rice, Silk, and Silt: Environment and Economy in Late Imperial South China*. Cambridge: Cambridge University Press, 1998.

104 Yi-Fu Tuan, *China*. Chicago: Aldine, 1969.

105 Lester J. Bilsky, "Ecological Crisis and Response in Ancient China," *Historical Ecology: Essays on Environment and Social Change*, edited by Lester J. Bilsky. Port Washington, NY: Kennikat Press, 1980, pp. 60–70.

106 Chris Coggins, *The Tiger and the Pangolin: Nature, Culture, and Conservation in China.* Honolulu: University of Hawai'i Press, 2003.

107 Conrad Totman, *A History of Japan.* Second edition. Oxford: Blackwell, 2005; *The Green Archipelago: Forestry in Preindustrial Japan.* Berkeley and Los Angeles, CA: University of California Press, 1989. Brett L. Walker, *The Conquest of Ainu Lands: Ecology and Culture in Japanese Expansion, 1590–1800.* Berkeley and Los Angeles, CA: University of California Press, 2001.

108 Libby Robin and Tom Griffiths, "Environmental History in Australasia," *Environment and History* 10, 4 (November 2004): 439–74.

109 Don Garden, *Australia, New Zealand, and the Pacific: An Environmental History.* Santa Barbara, CA: ABC-CLIO, 2005; Eric Pawson and Stephen Dovers, "Environmental History and the Challenges of Interdisciplinarity: An Antipodean Perspective," *Environment and History* 9, 1 (February 2003): 53–75.

110 *Environment and History*, special issue: "Australia," 4, 2 (June 1998); special issue: "New Zealand," 9, 4 (November 2003).

111 Tim Flannery, *The Future Eaters.*

112 Robin and Griffiths, "Environmental History in Australia," p. 459.

113 Stephen Dovers (ed.), *Australian Environmental History: Essays and Cases.* Melbourne: Oxford University Press, 1994; *Environmental History and Policy: Still Settling Australia.* Melbourne: Oxford University Press, 2000.

114 Geoffrey Bolton, *Spoils and Spoilers: A History of Australians Shaping Their Environment, 1788–1980.* Sydney: Allen and Unwin, 1992. First edition, 1981.

115 Eric Rolls, *A Million Wild Acres.* Melbourne: Nelson, 1981; *They All Ran Wild: The Story of Pests on the Land in Australia.* Sydney: Angus and Robertson, 1984. First edition, 1969; *Australia: A Biography*, Vol. I: *The Beginnings.* St Lucia: University of Queensland Press, 2000.

116 J. M. Powell, *A Historical Geography of Modern Australia: The Restive Fringe.* Cambridge: Cambridge University Press, 1988.

117 John Dargavel, *Fashioning Australia's Forests.* Melbourne: Oxford University Press, 1995.

118 Canberra: CRES (Centre for Resource and Environmental Studies, Australian National University), 1988, 1993,

1997, 1999, 2002. Melbourne: Oxford University Press, 1995.

119 Tom Griffiths, *Forests of Ash: An Environmental History.* Cambridge: Cambridge University Press, 2001.

120 Stephen J. Pyne, *Burning Bush: A Fire History of Australia.* New York: Henry Holt, 1991.

121 Tim Bonyhady, *Places Worth Keeping: Conservationists, Politics, and Law.* St Leonards, NSW: Allen and Unwin, 1993.

122 Libby Robin, *Defending the Little Desert: The Rise of Ecological Consciousness in Australia.* Melbourne: Melbourne University Press, 2000.

123 Drew Hutton and Libby Connors, *A History of the Australian Environmental Movement.* Melbourne: Cambridge University Press, 1999.

124 Tim Bonyhady, *The Colonial Earth.* Carleton: Miegunyah Press, 2000.

125 Eric Pawson and Tom Brooking, *Environmental Histories of New Zealand.* Melbourne: Oxford University Press, 2002.

126 James Belich, *Making Peoples: A History of the New Zealanders from Polynesian Settlement to the End of the Nineteenth Century.* Auckland: Penguin Press, 1996; *Paradise Reforged: A History of the New Zealanders from the 1880s to the Year 2000.* Honolulu: University of Hawai'i Press, 2001.

127 Michael King, *The Penguin History of New Zealand.* Auckland: Penguin Books, 2003.

128 Helen M. Leach, *1,000 Years of Gardening in New Zealand.* Wellington: A. H. and A. W. Reed, 1984.

129 Geoff Park, *Ngā Uruora.* Wellington, NZ: Victoria University Press, 1995. Alfred M. Crosby, *Ecological Imperialism: The Biological Expansion of Europe, 900–1900.* Cambridge: University of Cambridge Press, 2004. First edition, 1986.

130 J. R. McNeill (ed.), *Environmental History in the Pacific World.* Aldershot: Ashgate, 2001.

131 John Dargavel, Kay Dixon, and Noel Semple (eds), *Changing Tropical Forests: Historical Perspectives on Today's Challenges in Asia, Australasia and Oceania.* Canberra: Australian National University, 1988.

132 J. R. McNeill "Of Rats and Men: A Synoptic Environmental History of the Island Pacific," *Journal of World History,* 5 (1994), 299–349. Also appears in J. R. McNeill (ed.), *Environmental History in the Pacific World,* pp. 69–120.

133 Patrick V. Kirch and Terry L. Hunt (eds), *Historical Ecology in the Pacific Islands*. New Haven, CT: Yale University Press, 1997. Patrick V. Kirch, "The Environmental History of Oceanic Islands," pp. 1–21.

134 Paul D'Arcy, *The People of the Sea: Environment, Identity, and History in Oceania*. Honolulu: University of Hawai'i Press, 2005.

135 Jared Diamond, *Collapse: How Societies Choose to Fail or Succeed*. New York: Viking, 2005. "Twilight at Easter," pp. 79–119.

136 John Flenley and Paul Bahn, *The Enigmas of Easter Island: Island on the Edge*. Oxford: Oxford University Press, 2003.

137 Carl N. McDaniel and John M. Gowdy, *Paradise for Sale: A Parable of Nature*. Berkeley and Los Angeles, CA: University of California Press, 2000.

138 Jane Carruthers, "Africa: Histories, Ecologies, and Societies," *Environment and History* 10, 4 (November 2004): 379–406.

139 David Anderson and Richard Grove (eds), *Conservation in Africa: People, Policies, and Practice*. Cambridge: Cambridge University Press, 1987.

140 William Beinart, *The Rise of Conservation in South Africa: Settlers, Livestock, and the Environment, 1770–1950*. Oxford: Oxford University Press, 2003.

141 James C. McCann, *Green Land, Brown Land, Black Land: An Environmental History of Africa, 1800–1990*. Portsmouth, NH: Heinemann, 1999.

142 Helge Kjejkshus, *Ecology Control and Economic Development in East African History*. Berkeley and Los Angeles, CA: University of California Press, 1977.

143 Jane Carruthers, *The Kruger National Park: A Social and Political History*. Pietermaritzburg: University of Natal Press, 1995.

144 Clark C. Gibson, "Killing Animals with Guns and Ballots: The Political Economy of Zambian Wildlife Policy," *Environmental History Review*, 19 (1995), 49–75.

145 *Environmental History*, special issue, "Africa and Environmental History," 4, 2 (April 1999).

146 Farieda Khan, "Soil Wars: The Role of the African Soil Conservation Association in South Africa, 1953–1959," *Environmental History* 2, 4 (October 1997): 439–59.

147 *Environment and History*, special issue, "Zimbabwe," edited by Richard Grove and JoAnn McGregor, 1, 3 (October 1995).

148   The URL of this Internet site as of August 2005 is
      <www.stanford.edu/group/LAEH>.
149   ASEH website, August 2005 <www.h-net.org/~environ/
      historiography/latinam.htm>.
150   Guillermo Castro Herrera, *Los Trabajos de Ajuste y
      Combate: Naturaleza y sociedad en la historia de América
      Latina* (*The Labors of Conflict and Settlement: Nature and
      Society in the History of Latin America*). Bogotá/La Habana:
      CASA/Colcultura, 1995.
151   Nicolo Gligo and Jorge Morello, "Notas sobre la historia
      ecológica de América Latina" ("Studies on History and Envi-
      ronment in America"), in *Estilos de Desarrollo y Medio
      Ambiente en América Latina* (*Styles of Development and
      Environment in Latin America*), edited by O. Sunkel and
      N. Gligo, Mexico City: Fondo de Cultura Económica, El
      Trimestre Económico, 36, 2 t., 1980.
152   Luis Vitale, *Hacia una Historia del Ambiente en América
      Latina* (*Toward a History of the Environment in Latin
      America*). Mexico City: Nueva Sociedad/Editorial Nueva
      Imagen, 1983.
153   Bernardo García Martínez and Alba González Jácome (eds),
      *Estudios sobre Historia y Ambiente en América, I: Argen-
      tina, Bolivia, México, Paraguay* (*Studies on History and
      Environment in America, I: Argentina, Bolivia, Mexico,
      Paraguay*). Mexico City: Instituto Panamericano de
      Geografía e Historia/El Colegio de México, 1999.
154   Fernando Ortiz Monasterio, Isabel Fernández, Alicia
      Castillo, José Ortiz Monasterio, and Alfonso Bulle Goyri,
      Tierra Profanada: Historia Ambiental de México (*A
      Profaned Land: An Environmental History of Mexico*).
      Mexico City: Instituto Nacional de Antropología e
      Historia, Secretaría de Desarrollo Urbano y Ecología, 1987.
      Antonio E. Brailovsky and Dina Foguelman, *Memoria
      Verde: Historia ecológica de la Argentina* (*Green Memory:
      An Ecological History of Argentina*). Buenos Aires:
      Debolsillo, 2004.
155   Alfred W. Crosby, *The Columbian Exchange: Biological and
      Cultural Consequences of 1492*. Westport, CT: Greenwood
      Press, 1972. Republication with new material, Westport, CT:
      Praeger Publishers, 2003.
156   Elinor G. K. Melville, *A Plague of Sheep: Environmental
      Consequences of the Conquest of Mexico*. Cambridge: Cam-
      bridge University Press, 1994. Also in Spanish: Elinor G. K.
      Melville, *Plaga de Ovejas: Consecuencias ambientales de*

la conquista de México. Mexico City: Fondo de Cultura Económica, 1999.

157 Warren Dean, *With Broadax and Firebrand: The Destruction of the Brazilian Atlantic Forest.* Berkeley and Los Angeles, CA: University of California Press, 1995.

158 Warren Dean, *Brazil and the Struggle for Rubber: A Study in Environmental History.* Cambridge: Cambridge University Press, 2002. First edition, 1987.

159 Richard Charles Hoffmann, *Fishers' Craft and Lettered Art: Tracts on Fishing from the End of the Middle Ages.* Toronto: University of Toronto Press, 1997; and *Land, Liberties and Lordship in a Late Medieval Countryside: Agrarian Structures and Change in the Duchy of Wroclaw.* Philadelphia, PA: University of Pennsylvania Press, 1989; William TeBrake, *Medieval Frontier: Culture and Ecology in Rijnland.* College Station, TX: Texas A. & M. University Press, 1985; Petra J. E. M. van Dam, "De tanden van de waterwolf: Turfwinning en het onstaan van het Haarlemmermeer, 1350–1550" (The Teeth of the Waterwolf: Peat Cutting and the Increase of the Peat Lakes in the Rhineland, 1350–1550), *Tijdschrift voor Waterstaatsgeschiedenis,* 1996, 2, 81–92, with a summary in English; Charles R. Bowlus, "Ecological Crises in Fourteenth Century Europe," in *Historical Ecology: Essays on Environment and Social Change,* edited by Lester J. Bilsky, Port Washington, NY: National University Publications, Kennikat Press, 1980, pp. 86–99; Ronald E. Zupko and Robert A. Laures, *Straws in the Wind: Medieval Urban Environmental Law – The Case of Northern Italy.* Boulder, CO: Westview Press, 1996.

160 J. Donald Hughes, *Pan's Travail: Environmental Problems of the Ancient Greeks and Romans.* Baltimore, MD: Johns Hopkins University Press, 1994.

161 Russell Meiggs, *Trees and Timber in the Ancient Mediterranean World.* Oxford: Clarendon Press, 1982; Robert Sallares, *The Ecology of the Ancient Greek World.* Ithaca, NY: Cornell University Press, 1991; Thomas W. Gallant, *Risk and Survival in Ancient Greece: Reconstructing the Rural Domestic Economy.* Stanford, CA: Stanford University Press, 1991; Günther E. Thüry, *Die Wurzeln unserer Umweltkrise und die griechisch-römische Antike.* Salzburg: Otto Müller Verlag, 1995; Helmut Bender, "Historical Environmental Research from the Viewpoint of Provincial Roman Archaeology," in *Evaluation of Land Surfaces Cleared from Forests in the Mediterranean Region during the Time of the*

Roman Empire, edited by Burkhard Frenzel. Stuttgart: Gustav Fischer Verlag, 1994, pp. 145–56; Karl-Wilhelm Weeber, *Smog über Attika: Umweltverhalten im Altertum*. Zurich: Artemis Verlag, 1990; J. V. Thirgood, *Man and the Mediterranean Forest*. London: Academic Press, 1981.

Chapter 5 Global Environmental History

1 The phrase is taken from the title of Joel Tarr, *The Search for the Ultimate Sink: Urban Pollution in Historical Perspective*. Akron, OH: Akron University Press, 1996.

2 William L. Thomas, Jr. (ed.), *Man's Role in Changing the Face of the Earth*. Chicago: University of Chicago Press, 1956; William Moy Stratton Russell, *Man, Nature, and History: Controlling the Environment*. New York: Natural History Press for the American Museum of Natural History, 1969.

3 B. L. Turner, William C. Clark, Robert W. Kates, John F. Richards, Jessica T. Mathews, and William B. Meyer (eds), *The Earth as Transformed by Human Action: Global and Regional Changes in the Biosphere over the Past 300 Years*. Cambridge: Cambridge University Press, 1990.

4 Alfred W. Crosby, *The Columbian Exchange: Biological and Cultural Consequences of 1492*. Westport, CT: Greenwood Press, 1972. Republication with new material, Westport, CT: Praeger Publishers, 2003.

5 Alfred W. Crosby, *Ecological Imperialism: The Biological Expansion of Europe, 900–1900*. Cambridge: Cambridge University Press, 2004. First edition, 1986. See also his *Germs, Seeds, and Animals: Studies in Ecological History*. Armonk, NY: M. E. Sharpe, 1994.

6 Arnold Joseph Toynbee, *Mankind and Mother Earth: A Narrative History of the World*. New York: Oxford University Press, 1976.

7 Arnold Joseph Toynbee, *A Study of History*, 12 vols. London: Oxford University Press, 1934–61.

8 I. G. Simmons, *Changing the Face of the Earth: Culture, Environment, History*. Oxford: Blackwell, 1989; *Environmental History: A Concise Introduction*. Oxford: Blackwell, 1993.

9 Andrew Goudie, *The Human Impact on the Natural Environment*. Cambridge, MA: MIT Press, 1990.

10 Annette Manion, *Global Environmental Change: A Natural and Cultural History*. Harlow: Longman, 1991.

11 Stephen Boyden, *Biohistory: The Interplay between Human Society and the Biosphere*. Paris: UNESCO, 1992.

12 Jared Diamond, *Guns, Germs, and Steel: The Fates of Human Societies*. New York: W. W. Norton, 1997.

13 Jared Diamond, *Collapse: How Societies Choose to Fail or Succeed*. New York: Viking, 2005.

14 Clive Ponting, *A Green History of the World: The Environment and the Collapse of Great Civilizations*. New York: St. Martin's Press, 1991.

15 Mark Cioc, Björn-Ola Linnér, and Matt Osborn, "Environmental History Writing in Northern Europe," *Environmental History* 5, 3 (July 2000): 396–406. This is a suggestive survey of environmental history writing, on which this paragraph is based.

16 Sverker Sörlin and Anders Öckerman, *Jorden en Ö: En Global Miljöhistoria* (*Earth an Island: A Global Environmental History*). Stockholm: Natur och Kultur, 1998.

17 Hilde Ibsen, *Menneskets fotavtrykk: En oekologisk verdenshistorie*. Oslo: Tano Aschehoug, 1997.

18 Joachim Radkau, *Natur und Macht: Eine Weltgeschichte der Umwelt*. Munich: C. H. Beck, 2000.

19 J. Donald Hughes, *An Environmental History of the World: Humankind's Changing Role in the Community of Life*. London and New York: Routledge, 2001.

20 Sing C. Chew, *World Ecological Degradation: Accumulation, Urbanization, and Deforestation, 3000 B.C.–A.D. 2000*. Walnut Creek, CA: Rowman and Littlefield, 2001.

21 Ibid., p. 172.

22 Lester J. Bilsky (ed.), *Historical Ecology: Essays on Environment and Social Change*. Port Washington, NY: Kennikat Press, 1980.

23 Donald Worster (ed.), *The Ends of the Earth: Perspectives on Modern Environmental History*. Cambridge: Cambridge University Press, 1988.

24 Ibid., pp. 289–308.

25 J. Donald Hughes (ed.) *The Face of the Earth: Environment and World History*. Armonk, NY: M. E. Sharpe, 2000.

26 John R. McNeill, *Something New Under the Sun: An Environmental History of the Twentieth-Century World*. New York: W. W. Norton, 2000.

27 Ibid., p. 4.

28 John F. Richards, *The Unending Frontier: The Environmental History of the Early Modern World*. Berkeley and Los Angeles, CA: University of California Press, 2003.

29 Robert B. Marks, *The Origins of the Modern World: A Global and Ecological Narrative*. Lanham, MD: Rowman and Littlefield, 2002.

30 Ibid., p. 151.

31 Michael Williams, *Deforesting the Earth: From Prehistory to Global Crisis*. Chicago: University of Chicago Press, 2003.

32 Ibid., pp. 221, 446.

33 Richard P. Tucker and John F. Richards (eds), *Global Deforestation and the Nineteenth-Century World Economy*. Durham, NC: Duke University, 1983.

34 Leslie E. Sponsel, Thomas N. Headland, and Robert C. Bailey (eds), *Tropical Deforestation: The Human Dimension*. New York: Columbia University Press, 1996.

35 Stephen J. Pyne, *World Fire: The Culture of Fire on Earth*. New York: Holt, 1995. Pyne also has a number of regional studies on the subject of fire.

36 Richard H. Grove and John Chappell (eds), *El Niño: History and Crisis*. Cambridge: The White Horse Press, 2000.

37 Alfred W. Crosby, *Ecological Imperialism: The Biological Expansion of Europe, 900–1900*. Cambridge: Cambridge University Press, 2004. First edition, 1986.

38 Richard H. Grove, *Green Imperialism: Colonial Expansion, Tropical Island Edens and the Origins of Environmentalism, 1600–1860*. Cambridge: Cambridge University Press, 1995.

39 Peder Anker, *Imperial Ecology: Environmental Order in the British Empire, 1895–1945*. Cambridge, MA: Harvard University Press, 2001.

40 Richard Drayton, *Nature's Government: Science, Imperial Britain, and the "Improvement" of the World*. New Haven, CT: Yale University Press, 2000.

41 Deepak Kumar, *Science and the Raj, 1857–1905*. Delhi: Oxford University Press, 1995.

42 John M. MacKenzie, *Empires of Nature and the Nature of Empires: Imperialism, Scotland and the Environment*. East Linton: Tuckwell Press, 1997.

43 Tom Griffiths and Libby Robin (eds), *Ecology and Empire: Environmental History of Settler Societies*. Edinburgh: Keele University Press, 1997.

44 Richard P. Tucker, *Insatiable Appetite: The United States and the Ecological Degradation of the Tropical World*. Berkeley and Los Angeles, CA: University of California Press, 2000.

45 Thomas Dunlap, *Nature and the English Diaspora: Environment and History in the United States, Canada, Australia,*

and New Zealand. Cambridge: Cambridge University Press, 1999.

46 Ramachandra Guha, *Environmentalism: A Global History.* New York: Longman, 2000.

47 John McCormick, *Reclaiming Paradise: The Global Environmental Movement.* Bloomington, IN: Indiana University Press, 1989.

48 Carolyn Merchant, *Radical Ecology: The Search for a Livable World.* New York: Routledge, 1992.

49 John R. McNeill, *Something New Under the Sun*, p. 3.

50 Richard W. Bulliet, Pamela Kyle Crossley, Daniel R. Headrick, Steven W. Hirsch, Lyman L. Johnson, and David Northrup, *The Earth and Its Peoples: A Global History.* Boston: Houghton Mifflin, 1997, is one text that adopts environment, along with technology, as a consistent theme.

51 Harry J. Carroll, Jr., et al., *The Development of Civilization: A Documentary History of Politics, Society, and Thought* Chicago: Scott, Foresman, 1962, 2 vols., to give one example. It might be countered that the word is used innocently in a general sense, but for an analysis of the role of rhetoric, and the use of the word "development" in political discourse, see M. Jimmie Killingsworth and Jacqueline S. Palmer, *Ecospeak: Rhetoric and Environmental Politics in America*, Carbondale, IL: Southern Illinois University Press, 1992, particularly p. 9, where "developmentalists" are defined as those "who seek short-term economic gain regardless of the long-term environmental costs."

52 For the first two authors and colleagues, see Robert Costanza, John Cumberland, Herman Daly, Robert Goodland, and Richard Norgaard, *An Introduction to Ecological Economics.* Boca Raton, FL: St. Lucie Press, 1997; and Thomas Prugh, Robert Costanza, John H. Cumberland, Herman E. Daly, Robert Goodland, and Richard B. Norgaard, *Natural Capital and Human Economic Survival.* Boca Raton, FL: Lewis Publishers, 1999; others are Hilary French, *Vanishing Borders: Protecting the Planet in the Age of Globalization.* New York: W. W. Norton, 2000; James O'Connor, "Is Sustainable Capitalism Possible?" in *Is Capitalism Sustainable?: Political Economy and the Politics of Ecology*, edited by Martin O'Connor. New York: Guilford Press, 1994, pp. 152–75; and "The Second Contradiction of Capitalism," in *Natural Causes: Essays in Ecological Marxism*, by James O'Connor. New York: Guilford Press, 1998.

Chapter 6 Issues and Directions in Environmental History

1 Donald Worster, "The Two Cultures Revisited: Environmental History and the Environmental Sciences," *Environment and History* 2, 1 (February 1996): 3–14.

2 Steven Pyne, "Environmental History without Historians," *Environmental History* 10, 1 (January 2005): 72–4. The quotation is on p. 72.

3 John Opie, "Environmental History: Pitfalls and Opportunities," *Environmental Review* 7, 1 (Spring 1983): 8–16.

4 Jared Diamond, *Collapse: How Societies Choose to Fail or Succeed*. New York: Viking, 2005, p. 16.

5 J. R. McNeill, "Observations on the Nature and Culture of Environmental History," *History and Theory* 42 (December 2003): 5–43, p. 34.

6 William Cronon, "The Uses of Environmental History," *Environmental History Review* 17, 3 (Fall 1993): 1–22.

7 Donald Worster, *The Wealth of Nature: Environmental History and the Ecological Imagination*. New York: Oxford University Press, 1993.

8 Ibid., p. 63.

9 William Cronon (ed.), *Uncommon Ground: Toward Reinventing Nature*. New York: W. W. Norton, 1995.

10 Ibid., p. 70.

11 J. Donald Hughes, *Pan's Travail: Environmental Problems of the Ancient Greeks and Romans*. Baltimore, MD: Johns Hopkins University Press, 1994, pp. 73, 149.

12 Alfred W. Crosby, *The Columbian Exchange: Biological and Cultural Consequences of 1492*. Westport, CT: Greenwood Press, 1972. Republication with new material, Westport, CT: Praeger Publishers, 2003.

13 See Donald Worster, "The Vulnerable Earth: Toward a Planetary History," in *The Ends of the Earth: Perspectives on Modern Environmental History*. Cambridge: Cambridge University Press, 1988, pp. 3–22, and "Doing Environmental History," in ibid., pp. 289–308.

14 Elinor Melville, *A Plague of Sheep: Environmental Consequences of the Conquest of Mexico*. Cambridge: Cambridge University Press, 1997, p. 17.

15 Warren Dean, *With Broadax and Firebrand: The Destruction of the Brazilian Atlantic Forest*. Berkeley and Los Angeles, CA: University of California Press, 1995.

16 H. G. Wells, *The Outline of History*, 2 vols. New York: Macmillan, 1920.

17 Chris H. Lewis, "Telling Stories about the Future: Environmental History and Apocalyptic Science," *Environmental History Review* 17, 3 (Fall 1993): 43–60.

18 Carolyn Merchant, "The Theoretical Structure of Ecological Revolutions," *Environmental Review* 11, 4 (Winter 1987): 265–74; Carolyn Merchant, *Ecological Revolutions: Nature, Gender, and Science in New England*. Chapel Hill, NC: University of North Carolina Press, 1989.

19 Madhav Gadgil and Ramachandra Guha, "A Theory of Ecological History," Part I of *This Fissured Land: An Ecological History of India*. Berkeley and Los Angeles, CA: University of California Press, 1992, pp. 9–68.

20 James O'Connor, "What Is Environmental History? Why Environmental History?" in *Natural Causes: Essays in Ecological Marxism,* edited by James O'Connor. New York and London: The Guilford Press, 1998, pp. 48–70.

21 James O'Connor, "The Second Contradiction of Capitalism," in *Natural Causes: Essays in Ecological Marxism,* edited by James O'Connor. New York and London: The Guilford Press, 1998, pp. 158–77.

22 James O'Connor, "Culture, Nature, and the Materialist Conception of History," in *Natural Causes: Essays in Ecological Marxism*, edited by James O'Connor. New York and London: The Guilford Press, 1998, pp. 29–47. The quotation is on p. 43.

23 O'Connor, "What is Environmental History?", pp. 65–6.

24 "What's Next for Environmental History?" *Environmental History* 10, 1 (January 2005): 30–109.

25 J. R. McNeill, "Observations on the Nature and Culture of Environmental History," *History and Theory* 42 (December 2003): 5–43, especially pp. 42–3.

26 Björn-Ola Linnér, *The Return of Malthus: Environmentalism and Post-War Population-Resource Crises*. Stroud, UK: White Horse Press, 2004.

27 Otis L. Graham, Jr., *A Limited Bounty: The United States Since World War II*. New York: McGraw-Hill, 1995.

28 Carl N. McDaniel and John M. Gowdy, *Paradise for Sale: A Parable of Nature*. Berkeley and Los Angeles, CA: University of California Press, 2000.

29 Michael Williams, *Deforesting the Earth: From Prehistory to Global Crisis*. Chicago: University of Chicago Press, 2003, pp. 203–4.

30   John F. Richards, *The Unending Frontier: The Environmental History of the Early Modern World*. Berkeley and Los Angeles, CA: University of California Press, 2003.
31   Anthony B. Anderson, Peter H. May, and Michael J. Balick, *The Subsidy from Nature: Palm Forests, Peasantry, and Development on an Amazon Frontier*. New York: Columbia University Press, 1991.
32   Edmund Russell, "Evolutionary History: Prospectus for a New Field," *Environmental History* 8, 2 (April 2003): 204–28.
33   Peter R. Grant, *Ecology and Evolution of Darwin's Finches*. Princeton, NJ: Princeton University Press, 1986.
34   In this regard, see a book by a biologist, Stephen R. Palumbi, *The Evolution Explosion: How Humans Cause Rapid Evolutionary Change*. New York: W. W. Norton, 2001.
35   Lance van Sittert, "The Other Seven-Tenths," *Environmental History* 10, 1 (January 2005): 106–9.
36   Fernand Braudel, *The Mediterranean and the Mediterranean World in the Age of Philip II*, trans. Siân Reynolds. New York: Harper & Row, 1972. First edition, 1949.
37   Arthur F. McEvoy, *The Fisherman's Problem: Ecology and Law in the California Fisheries, 1850–1980*. Cambridge: Cambridge University Press, 1986.
38   E. Stroud, "Does Nature Always Matter? Following Dirt Through History," *History and Theory* 42 (2003): 75–81.

Chapter 7   Thoughts on Doing Environmental History

1   Donald Worster, "Appendix: Doing Environmental History," in *The Ends of the Earth: Perspectives on Modern Environmental History*, edited by Donald Worster. Cambridge: Cambridge University Press, 1988, pp. 289–307.
2   Carolyn Merchant, *The Columbia Guide to American Environmental History*. New York: Columbia University Press, 2002.
3   Accessible, and available for download, at Merchant's site: <www.cnr.berkeley.edu/departments/espm/env-hist>, as of September, 2005.
4   William Cronon, "A Place for Stories: Nature, History, and Narrative," *Journal of American History* 78 (March 1992): 1347–76.
5   I. G. Simmons, *Environmental History: A Concise Introduction*. Oxford: Blackwell, 1993.

6 Donald Worster, "Appendix: Doing Environmental History," pp. 290–1.
7 Ibid., p. 302.
8 Ibid., p. 306.
9 Carolyn Merchant, "Introduction," in *Columbia Guide to American Environmental History*, p. xv.
10 William Cronon, "A Place for Stories," p. 1372.
11 Ibid.
12 Ibid., p. 1373.
13 I. G. Simmons, *Environmental History*, p. 55.
14 Ibid., p. 188.
15 Ari Kelman, *A River and Its City: The Nature of Landscape in New Orleans*. Berkeley and Los Angeles, CA: University of California Press, 2003.
16 Craig E. Colten, *An Unnatural Metropolis: Wresting New Orleans from Nature*. Baton Rouge: Louisiana State University Press, 2004.
17 <www.lib.duke.edu/forest/Research/databases.html>.
18 <www.eseh.organization/bibliography.html>.
19 <www.lib.duke.edu/forest/Events/ICEHO>.
20 <www.h-net.org/~environ/>.
21 J. R. McNeill, "Observations on the Nature and Culture of Environmental History," *History and Theory* 42 (December 2003): 5–43. The quotation is on p. 42.
22 Alan H. R. Baker, *Geography and History: Bridging the Divide*. Cambridge: Cambridge University Press, 2003.
23 Craig E. Colten, "Historical Geography and Environmental History," and Michael Williams, "The End of Modern History?," *Geographical Review* 88, 2 (April 1998): iii–iv and 275–300.
24 Michael Williams, "The Relations of Environmental History and Historical Geography," *Journal of Historical Geography* 20, 1 (1994): 3–21.
25 Donald Worster, *Nature's Economy*. Cambridge: Cambridge University Press, 1977.
26 Frank Benjamin Golley, *A History of the Ecosystem Concept in Ecology: More Than the Sum of the Parts*. New Haven, CT: Yale University Press, 1993.

Select Bibliography

Baker, Alan H. R. *Geography and History: Bridging the Divide.* Cambridge: Cambridge University Press, 2003.

Bao Maohong. "Environmental History in China," *Environment and History* 10, 4 (November 2004): 475–99.

Beinart, William. "African History and Environmental History," *African Affairs* 99 (2000): 269–302.

—. *African History and Environmental History* (June 11, 2001). See American Society for Environmental History, *Historiography Series in Global Environmental History.* <www.h-net.org/~environ/historiography/historiography.html>.

Bess, Michael, Cioc, Mark, and Sievert, James. "Environmental History Writing in Southern Europe," *Environmental History* 5, 4 (October 2000): 545–56.

Bird, Elizabeth Ann R. "The Social Construction of Nature: Theoretical Approaches to the History of Environmental Problems," *Environmental Review* 11, 4 (Winter 1987): 255–64.

Blum, Elizabeth D. "Linking American Women's History and Environmental History: A Preliminary Historiography." <www.h-net.org/~environ/historiography/uswomen.htm>.

Carruthers, Jane. "Environmental History in Southern Africa: An Overview," in *South Africa's Environmental History: Cases and Comparisons*, edited by Stephen Dovers, Ruth Edgecombe, and Bill Guest. Athens, OH: Ohio University Press, 2003, pp. 3–18.

—. "Africa: Histories, Ecologies and Societies," *Environment and History* 10, 4 (November 2004): 379–406.

Cioc, Mark, Linnér, Björn-Ola, and Osborn, Matt. "Environmental History Writing in Northern Europe," *Environmental History* 5, 3 (July 2000): 396–406.

Coates, Peter. "Clio's New Greenhouse," *History Today* 46, 8 (August 1996): 15–22.

—. "Emerging from the Wilderness (or, from Redwoods to Bananas): Recent Environmental History in the United States and the Rest of the Americas," *Environment and History* 10, 4 (November 2004): 407–38.

Colten, Craig E. "Historical Geography and Environmental History," *Geographical Review* 88 (1998): iii–iv.

Cronon, William. "A Place for Stories: Nature, History, and Narrative," *The Journal of American History* 78, 4 (March 1992): 1347–76.

—. "The Uses of Environmental History," *Environmental History Review* 17, 3 (Fall 1993): 1–22.

Crosby, Alfred W. "The Past and Present of Environmental History," *American Historical Review* 100, 4 (October 1995): 1177–89.

Demeritt, David. "The Nature of Metaphors in Cultural Geography and Environmental History," *Progress in Human Geography* 18 (1994): 163–85.

Dovers, Stephen. "Australian Environmental History: Introduction, Reviews and Principles," in *Australian Environmental History: Essays and Cases*, edited by Stephen Dovers. Oxford: Oxford University Press, 1994, pp. 1–20.

—. "Sustainability and 'Pragmatic' Environmental History: A Note from Australia," *Environmental History Review* 18, 3 (Fall 1994): 21–36.

—. "On the Contribution of Environmental History to Current Debate and Policy," *Environment and History* 6, 2 (May 2000): 131–50.

Dovers, Stephen, Edgecombe, Ruth, and Guest, Bill (eds). *South Africa's Environmental History: Cases and Comparisons.* Athens, OH: Ohio University Press, 2003, pp. 3–18.

Fay, Brian. "Environmental History: Nature at Work," *History and Theory* 42 (December 2003) 1–4.

Flanagan, Maureen A. "Environmental Justice in the City: A Theme for Urban Environmental History," *Environmental History* 5, 2 (April 2000): 159–64.

Garden, Don. "Where Are the Historians?" *Australian Environmental History* (October 11, 2000). See American Society for Environmental History, *Historiography Series in Global Environmental History.* <www.h-net.org/~environ/historiography/historiography.html>.

Green, William A. "Environmental History," in *History, Historians, and the Dynamics of Change*, edited by William A. Green. Westport, CT: Praeger, 1993, pp. 167–90.

Grove, Richard. "Environmental History," in *New Perspectives in Historical Writing*, edited by Peter Burke. Cambridge: Polity, 2001, pp. 261–82.

Hays, Samuel P. *Explorations in Environmental History.* Pittsburgh, PA: University of Pittsburgh Press, 1998.

—. "Toward Integration in Environmental History," *Pacific Historical Review* 70, 1 (2001): 59–68.

Herrera, Guillermo Castro. "The Environmental Crisis and the Tasks of History in Latin America," *Environment and History* 3, 1 (February 1997): 1–18.

—. "Environmental History (Made) in Latin America" (April 19, 2001). See American Society for Environmental History, *Historiography Series in Global Environmental History.* <www.h-net.org/~environ/historiography/historiography.html>.

Hughes, J. Donald. "Ecology and Development as Narrative Themes of World History," *Environmental History Review* 19, 1 (Spring 1995): 1–16.

—. "Environmental History – World," in *A Global Encyclopedia of Historical Writing*, 2 vols, edited by David R. Woolf, New York, Garland Publishing, 1998, Vol. 1, pp. 288–91.

—. "Global Dimensions of Environmental History," (Forum on Environmental History, Retrospect and Prospect) *Pacific Historical Review* 70, 1 (February 2001): 91–101.

—. "The Nature of Environmental History," *Revista de Historia Actual* (*Contemporary History Review*, Spain) 1, 1 (2003): 23–30.

—. "The Greening of World History," in *Palgrave Advances in World Histories*, edited by Marnie Hughes-Warrington. Houndmills and New York: Palgrave Macmillan, 2005, pp. 238–55.

Jacoby, Karl. "Class and Environmental History: Lessons from the War in the Adirondacks," *Environmental History* 2, 3 (July 1997): 324–42.

Jamieson, Duncan R. "American Environmental History," *CHOICE* 32, 1 (September 1994): 49–60.

Krech, Shepard, III, McNeill, J. R., and Merchant, Carolyn. *Encyclopedia of World Environmental History.* 3 vols. New York and London: Routledge, 2004.

Leach, Melissa and Green, Cathy. "Gender and Environmental History: From Representation of Women and Nature to Gender Analysis of Ecology and Politics," *Environment and History* 3, 3 (October 1997): 343–70.

Leibhardt, Barbara. "Interpretation and Causal Analysis: Theories in Environmental History." *Environmental Review* 12, 1 (1988): 23–36.

Lewis, Chris H. "Telling Stories About the Future: Environmental History and Apocalyptic Science," *Environmental History Review* 17, 3 (Fall 1993): 43–60.

Lowenthal, David. "Environmental History: From Genesis to Apocalypse," *History Today* 51, 4 (2001): 36–44.

McCann, James C. "Causation and Climate in African History" (September 25, 2000). See American Society for Environmental History, *Historiography Series in Global Environmental History*. <www.h-net.org/~environ/historiography/historiography. html>.

McNeill, John R. "Observations on the Nature and Culture of Environmental History," *History and Theory* 42 (December 2003): 5–43.

Melosi, Martin V. "Equity, Eco-Racism and Environmental History," *Environmental History Review* 19, 3 (Fall 1995): 1–16.

Merchant, Carolyn. *The Columbia Guide to American Environmental History*. New York: Columbia University Press, 2002.

—. "Shades of Darkness: Race and Environmental History," *Environmental History* 8, 3 (July 2003): 380–94.

Merricks, Linda. "Environmental History," *Rural History* 7 (1996): 97–106.

Mulvihill, Peter R., Baker, Douglas C., and Morrison, William R. "A Conceptual Framework for Environmental History in Canada's North," *Environmental History* 6, 4 (October 2001): 611–26.

Myllyntaus, Timo. "Writing about the Past with Green Ink: The Emergence of Finnish Environmental History, in *Skrifter fran forskningsprogrammet Landskapet som arena nr X*, edited by Erland Marald and Christer Nordlund. Umeå: Umeå University Press, 2003.

Nash, Roderick. "Environmental History," in *The State of American History*, edited by Herbert J. Bass. Chicago: Quadrangle Press, 1970, pp. 249–60.

—. "American Environmental History: A New Teaching Frontier," *Pacific Historical Review* 41, 3 (1972): 362–72.

Norwood, Vera. "Disturbed Landscape/Disturbing Process: Environmental History for the Twenty-First Century," *Pacific Historical Review* 70, 1 (February 2001): 77–90.

O'Connor, James. "What Is Environmental History? Why Environmental History?" in *Natural Causes: Essays in Ecological*

Marxism, edited by James O'Connor. New York and London: The Guilford Press, 1998, pp. 48–70.

Opie, John. "Environmental History: Pitfalls and Opportunities," *Environmental Review* 7, 1 (Spring 1983), 8–16.

Osborn, Matt. "Sowing the Field of British Environmental History" (September 19, 2001). See American Society for Environmental History, *Historiography Series in Global Environmental History*. <www.h-net.org/~environ/historiography/historiography. html>.

Pawson, Eric and Dovers, Stephen. "Environmental History and the Challenges of Interdisciplinarity: An Antipodean Perspective," *Environment and History* 9, 1 (February 2003): 53–75.

Powell, Joseph M. "Historical Geography and Environmental History: An Australian Interface," *Journal of Historical Geography* 22 (1996): 253–73.

Pyne, Steven. "Environmental History without Historians," *Environmental History* 10, 1 (January 2005): 72–4.

Rajan, S. Ravi. "The Ends of Environmental History: Some Questions," *Environment and History* 3, 2 (June 1997): 245–52.

Rakestraw, Lawrence. "Conservation Historiography: An Assessment," *Pacific Historical Review* 41, 3 (August 1972): 271–88.

Rangarajan, Mahesh. "Environmental Histories of South Asia: A Review Essay," *Environment and History* 2, 2 (June 1996): 129–43.

Robin, Libby and Griffiths, Tom. "Environmental History in Australasia," *Environment and History* 10, 4 (November 2004): 439–74.

Rome, Adam. "What Really Matters in History? Environmental Perspectives on Modern America," *Environmental History* 7, 2 (April 2002): 303–18.

— (ed.). "What's Next for Environmental History?" (An Anniversary Forum containing 29 short essays by scholars on future directions for environmental history), *Environmental History* 10, 1 (January 2005): 30–109.

Rothman, Hal. "A Decade in the Saddle: Confessions of a Recalcitrant Editor," *Environmental History* 7, 1 (January 2002): 9–21.

Russell, Edmund. "Evolutionary History: Prospectus for a New Field," *Environmental History* 8, 2 (April 2003): 204–28.

Russell, Emily Wyndham Barnett. *People and the Land Through Time: Linking Ecology and History*. New Haven, CT: Yale University Press, 1997.

Schatzki, Theodore R. "Nature and Technology in History," *History and Theory* 42 (December 2003): 82–93.

Sellers, Christopher. "Thoreau's Body: Towards an Embodied Environmental History," *Environmental History* 4, 4 (October 1999): 486–514.

Simmons, Ian Gordon. *Changing the Face of the Earth: Culture, Environment, History.* Oxford: Blackwell, 1989.

—. *Environmental History: A Concise Introduction.* Oxford: Oxford University Press, 1993.

Sörlin, Sverker and Warde, Paul. "The Problem of the Problem of Environmental History: A Re-Reading of the Field and Its Purpose," Centre for History and Economics, Kings College, University of Cambridge. See <www-histecon.kings.cam.ac.uk/ envdoc/docs/turkku_keynote_ warde_sorlin.pdf>.

Star, Paul. "New Zealand Environmental History: A Question of Attitudes," *Environment and History* 9, 4 (November 2003): 463–76.

Steinberg, Theodore. "Down to Earth: Nature, Agency and Power in History," *American Historical Review* 107, 3 (2002): 798–820.

Stewart, Mart A. "Environmental History: Profile of a Developing Field," *History Teacher* 31 (May 1998): 351–68.

—. "If John Muir Had Been an Agrarian: American Environmental History West and South," *Environment and History* 11, 2 (May 2005): 139–62.

Steyn, Phia. "A Greener Past? An Assessment of South African Environmental Historiography," *New Contree* 46 (November 1999): 7–27.

—. "The Greening of Our Past? An Assessment of South African Environmental Historiography" (November 13, 2000). See American Society for Environmental History, *Historiography Series in Global Environmental History.* <www.h-net.org/ ~environ/historiography/historiography.html>.

Stine, Jeffrey K. and Tarr, Joel A. "At the Intersection of Histories: Technology and the Environment," *Technology and Culture* 39 (October 1998): 601–40.

Stoll, Mark (ed.). American Society for Environmental History. *Historiography Series in Global Environmental History,* <www. h-net.org/~environ/historiography/historiography.html> (or access the American Society for Environmental History website under "Resources").

Stroud, Ellen. "Does Nature Always Matter? Following Dirt Through History," *History and Theory* 42 (December 2003) 75–81.

Sutter, Paul. "What Can U.S. Environmental Historians Learn from Non-U.S. Environmental Historiography?" *Environmental History* 8, 1 (January 2003): 109–29.

Tarr, Joel A. "Urban History and Environmental History in the United States" (November 30, 2000). See American Society for Environmental History, *Historiography Series in Global Environmental History.* <www.h-net.org/~environ/historiography/historiography.html>.

Tate, Thad W. "Problems of Definition in Environmental History," *American Historical Association Newsletter* (1981): 8–10.

Taylor, Alan. "Unnatural Inequalities: Social and Environmental Histories," *Environmental History* 1, 4 (October 1996): 6–19.

Terrie, Philip G. "Recent Work in Environmental History," *American Studies International* 27 (1989): 42–63.

Uekoetter, Frank. "Confronting the Pitfalls of Current Environmental History: An Argument for an Organizational Approach," *Environment and History* 4, 1 (February 1998): 31–52.

Weiner, Douglas R. "A Death-Defying Attempt to Articulate a Coherent Definition of Environmental History," *Environmental History* 10, 3 (July 2005): 404–20.

White, Richard. "American Environmental History: The Development of a New Historical Field," *Pacific Historical Review* 54 (August 1985): 297–335.

—. "Afterword, Environmental History: Watching a Historical Field Mature," *Pacific Historical Review* 70 (February 2001). 103–11.

Williams, Michael. "The Relations of Environmental History and Historical Geography," *Journal of Historical Geography* 20 (1984): 3–21.

—. "The End of Modern History?," *Geographical Review* 88, 2 (April 1998): 275–300.

Winiwarter, Verena, et al. "Environmental History in Europe from 1994 to 2004: Enthusiasm and Consolidation," *Environment and History* 10, 4 (November 2004): 501–30.

Worster, Donald. "World Without Borders: The Internationalizing of Environmental History," *Environmental Review* 6, 2 (Fall 1982): 8–13.

—. "History as Natural History: An Essay on Theory and Method," *Pacific Historical Review* 53 (1984): 1–19.

—. "Doing Environmental History," in *The Ends of the Earth: Perspectives on Modern Environmental History,* edited by Donald Worster. Cambridge: Cambridge University Press, 1988, pp. 289–307.

—. "Nature and the Disorder of History," *Environmental History Review* 18 (Summer 1994): 1–15.

—. "The Two Cultures Revisited: Environmental History and the Environmental Sciences," *Environment and History* 2, 1 (February 1996): 3–14.

Worster, Donald, et al. "A Roundtable: Environmental History," *Journal of American History* 74, 4 (March 1990): 1087–147.

Index

CPSIA information can be obtained at www.ICGtesting.com
Printed in the USA
BVOW03s0859151014

370830BV00013B/43/P